Demystifying Differentiation in Elementary School

Tools, Strategies, & Activities to Use NOW

Caroline Eidson, Bob Iseminger, Chris Taibbi

Pieces of Learning

CLC0429
© 2008 Pieces of Learning
Marion IL
ISBN 978-1-34358-11-5
Cover by John Steele

The Web Sites noted are correct as of the publication date. However, they may have become inactive or modified since that date.
We have made every effort to validate Web Site sources.

Table of Contents

INTRODUCTION

Why We Wrote This Book

Our work as teachers and educational consultants has given us the opportunity to meet many K through 12 educators across the country. It was with these professionals in mind that we first conceived of a book that would assist teachers in accomplishing what is, undoubtedly, a difficult proposition: addressing the diverse learning needs of each student within a single classroom. So, in February 2007, we were pleased when that book, <u>Demystifying Differentiation in Middle School</u>, was published.

The feedback we received from that publication told us two things. First, we had successfully responded to the question we each had been asked repeatedly as we delivered our workshops, namely: *"Where can I find a book that has a bunch of these kinds of activities already written for me to use in my classroom?"* It seemed that our book intended for middle school teachers had filled that niche nicely. The second thing we discovered, however, was that there was a need, in fact a *demand*, for a similar book that could assist teachers at the elementary level.

And so it is that this book has come to be. While there are many books available about curriculum differentiation, most of them address the theory and rationale behind it and discuss models and strategies that support it. Some of these books offer limited examples of differentiated tasks and activities. However, few provide comprehensive collections of activities that demonstrate how to use differentiation in different subject areas at a variety of grade levels in mixed-ability elementary classrooms. With this publication, we hope to add to the resources that are already available and to further elementary teachers' efforts toward differentiated classrooms.

Who This Book is For

Of course, this book is for all elementary school teachers and administrators who are looking for ways to make curriculum differentiation work in their classrooms. But in writing this book, we made a few assumptions about our audience. Because we didn't

With these assumptions in mind, we wrote this book for teachers and administrators who are ready to take differentiation to the next level in their classrooms and schools, who believe that differentiation works, and who are looking for more examples of it.

want to create *another* book about the basics of and rationale for differentiation, we first assumed that teachers reading this book would have some background with differentiation, perhaps through coursework and workshops or through their own reading and research. We also assumed that they buy into the idea of differentiation, that they realize the time and effort that it requires can mean greater learning for students, and that they also believe it is a valuable tool for meeting student needs in mixed-ability settings. We then assumed that our readers believe in the need for high expectations for all learners and are striving to challenge all students.

How to Use This Book

Any author who writes about instructional practices and strategies hopes that educators will take what is written on the page and adapt it to meet their own needs

and situations. And so it is with us. While we expect that teachers will use many of the activities and tasks just as they are presented, it is our hope that teachers will also use them as jumping-off points for creating their own differentiated lessons. Thus, we hope that this book empowers teachers first by doing much of the work of differentiation for them and second by encouraging through example the design and use of other differentiated activities and tasks.

To this end, we provided some background information for each activity presented. This information includes 1) a brief overview addressing any instructional or management issues related to the activity, 2) standards and objectives addressed, and 3) ideas for bringing closure to the lesson. Because we want teachers to adapt the activities as needed for the classes and grades they teach, we have not designated specific grade levels for them. Rather, we have offered a range of activities and topics in each subject area that are representative of elementary standards, benchmarks, and objectives in various states. It is our hope that this approach provides teachers and administrators with the flexibility either to use the differentiated activities as they are presented or to create their own using the tools and techniques provided in this book.

What Is Differentiation?
And Why Should We Be Doing It?

There are many ways of going forward,
but only one way of standing still.
Franklin D. Roosevelt

Consider for a moment the intimidating responsibilities associated with being a team sports coach. Even before the first game of the season is played, the coach will most certainly spend many hours observing her team in practice as they run through specific drills. She will watch and take notes as she learns more about her players' individual skills so that she can design a winning team. She will match players' skills to the field positions which will best highlight the players' strengths and downplay their weaknesses. And then, even as the season progresses, as games are won and lost, it will be that coach's job to ensure that every player's skills improve – for the good of the individual *and* the team. With the coach's careful and deliberate modeling, practice drills, and post-game analysis, the players begin to form a better understanding of the sport's strategy, and from bench warmer to star player, each builds on the skills he brought to the field that first day of practice.

> Our job as teachers in differentiated classrooms is like that of a coach. We have "players" who come to us with different skills, talents, and interests. It is the team we are given, and we must "win" with this team by making every player the best he can be and by finding where each one fits in our master plan for success. We must organize practices and activities that prepare each player for "game day." In the classroom that may be the "big test," but as any good coach knows, the real game is life. The experience students have in our classrooms should leave them not only with a better knowledge of our subject area, but also with information about themselves that they can use to be successful in other areas of school and in life.
>
> Social Studies teacher,
> North Carolina

In truth, thinking about athletics is an apt place to begin building an understanding of and rationale for curriculum differentiation. Not so sure of this statement? Let's try applying this same approach to our classrooms by asking these essential questions:

- What would classrooms look like if teachers, like the coach above, were able to determine their students' skills and talents early in the year?

- What would happen if they were able to continue to assess their students' growth in an ongoing manner throughout the year and then match students to learning tasks designed to improve their skills and talents?

- Moreover, what would classrooms look like if they focused on growth for all students regardless of their starting points?

The answer: *Those classrooms would look a lot like the outdoor classroom already created by our sports coach – they would be **differentiated**.*

There has been much attention paid to the topic of curriculum differentiation in recent years, as evidenced by hundreds of books, journal articles, and conference sessions with this topic in their titles. With this in mind, the goal of this chapter is to provide an overview of curriculum differentiation rather than an in-depth exploration of it. For those who are seeking a more thorough discussion of the topic, who crave more information, we recommend the fine work of Carol Ann Tomlinson and others who have established a long-standing reputation in the field of curriculum differentiation. Please see the *Resources* provided at the end of the book.

A Quick Look at the Basics of Differentiation

For just a moment, let's revisit our sports team and its coach. The season is now fully underway. While playing a game one evening, a player is injured. Seeing that the injury is quite possibly severe, the coach recommends that the player go to a doctor. At the doctor's office, the player is examined and is asked a series of questions, and his symptoms are evaluated. The point of all this probing is to help the doctor determine a diagnosis. Once the doctor reaches this stage, she outlines a series of recommended steps. She prescribes a medication and rest, and she arranges for physical therapy. The goal of the doctor's prescribed course of action is simple: to help the player recover from his specific type of injury.

Classroom differentiation is very much like the work that goes on in a doctor's office. Typically, a teacher may think to examine most critically only the needs of the students in terms of *readiness* or *ability*. But in a differentiated classroom, the teacher understands that students bring *much more* to the environment than just what they already know or are capable of picking up quickly. They also bring to the classroom a variety of learning profiles and interests.

Much like a doctor uses a wide variety of tests to determine the specific nature and severity of

> When teachers take measured, proactive steps to address needs in the classroom, they are differentiating their instruction.

the injury, teachers in differentiated classrooms use as much information as they can gather to design curriculum and instruction that provide both success and challenge for all their students. So, for example, while studying the solar system, a teacher might ask herself:

- *What would students be interested in learning more about, either individually or in small groups?*
- *Do some students benefit more from working in pairs or groups while others are at their best when working on their own?*

And of course,

- *How can students who already grasp much of the material being presented go further in their understanding, while other students can get the more basic information that they need?*

As a doctor moves from making a diagnosis to offering a plan for a patient's treatment, she can vary a number of items to meet the individual's needs. She might select a particular form of medication. She might recommend alterations in the patient's daily routine at home to speed recovery. She might even advise the patient to seek further assistance from another specialist. Just as there may be many courses of action to speed a patient's recovery, in terms of what can be differentiated in a classroom, the answer is simple: ***if a teacher can design it, it can be differentiated.*** A fairly simple way to analyze a teacher's options for differentiation is to consider the broad categories of content, process, and product. Certainly a teacher can differentiate what students will learn (content) by addressing different learning objectives, by focusing on concepts and generalizations that encourage different levels of understanding, and by providing a range of materials and resources.

Likewise, almost every learning objective has multiple ways that students can achieve it (process). So, for instance, some students can come to understand a topic by reading various articles about it while others can look at pictures or photographs related to it and draw their own conclusions, and still others can listen to music related to that same topic. Differentiating process asks teachers to provide a variety of different ways that students can make sense of a question, issue, or topic or develop a skill.

Finally, teachers who differentiate products look for many ways for students to show or explain what they have learned. These teachers might allow students to choose from a list of product options when completing independent studies or small group investigations. They might allow students to respond to information in different formats so that some students write about their understandings while others diagram or illustrate theirs. These teachers might even differentiate unit tests and quizzes, asking different questions depending on students' experiences and levels of growth throughout a unit.

Whether differentiating or not, it is safe to say that it is easier for a teacher to design constructive lessons and assessments and to measure student growth *when she knows ahead of time what her learning objectives are.* After all, a doctor's objective regarding her patient is straightforward: to affect a full and speedy recovery. A teacher's overall classroom objective, in broad strokes, should be similarly straightforward: to broaden the knowledge and skill sets of all of her students. At a more pragmatic level, the foundation of effective differentiation is clarity about what students should gain from a particular unit of study. So before beginning to differentiate instruction in a particular unit, teachers must establish their objectives for that unit. And once the unit has begun, they, like the coach at the beginning of this chapter, must keep their eyes on the ball, making sure that the resources they are providing and the tasks they are assigning directly address their objectives.

Once the learning objectives have been selected and classroom instructional opportunities have been designed, it is easy to place assessment on the back burner. After all, the teacher has already expended a great deal of energy! It is tempting to think of assessment as simply "the stuff that will come later – at the end of the unit." But in a successful, differentiated classroom, assessment in fact begins before the teaching of the unit and is an integral part of the planning process. Assessment becomes the basis for

teachers' decisions about what students need. It should be ongoing and

> **If a teacher can design it, it can be differentiated.**

varied, providing current information about students' progress. Chapter 12 addresses the important role of assessment.

The cycle of assessment and learning in a differentiated classroom provides both success and challenge for all learners so that all come to feel that they are working hard and that their hard work is paying off. No student should be made to feel incapable or unworthy because he lacks some prerequisites. Likewise, no student should find that his days are filled with busywork that requires little effort.

Good coaches ensure that their training is responsive to the players' needs. Differentiation is exactly the same, providing teachers with a framework that helps them take their learners as far as they can go as quickly as they can move.

The Rationale Behind Differentiation

Teaching is difficult. This is true whether you are teaching five-year-olds how to tie their shoes or nine-year-olds how to perform long division. And, frankly, differentiating curriculum and instruction does place additional demands on teachers' time and energy. But when learning is at stake, it is hard to argue against an approach that benefits students and ensures growth for all. Just as good doctors would never prescribe the same medication to all of their patients regardless of their differing symptoms, good teachers seeking to really meet their students' learning needs cannot expect that all will benefit from the same teaching.

Essentially, differentiation asks us to redefine what "fair" is in our classrooms. Does it mean that all students receive the same instruction, materials, and tasks? Or does it mean that all students receive the instruc-

tion, materials, and tasks that they **need** in order to maximize their learning? Those in favor of differentiation argue that it means the latter, that it is, in fact, highly unfair to teach in a "one size fits all" mode.

From a teacher perspective, once the management piece has been tackled and the basics have been grasped and practiced, differentiation can be both exciting and challenging. It tests our creativity and asks us to look at our work more critically as we evaluate our attempts to meet our students' needs. It creates a dynamic learning environment where the daily routine is driven not by a textbook or a pacing guide but by the needs and interests of the learners. The results can be exhilarating.

Is it more work? Yes.
Is it worth it? Absolutely.

Helpful Tools
for Differentiating Instruction

The tools that teachers have at their disposal in today's classrooms are much richer than the ones we might recall our teachers using during our own schooling. We now know significantly more about the brain and how it works than we did just twenty years ago. Not surprisingly, entirely new educational models have sprung up as educators reexamine their approaches to instruction in light of this dramatic increase in knowledge. With so many new ideas and directions to choose from, these new trends may feel exciting and invigorating. And yet a common concern teachers express is the sense of stress they feel as they are asked to implement so many initiatives, new or old, at any one given time. How can we, teachers ask, possibly know which ones will be really effective and which ones can really be put to use in the "real world" of our classrooms?

> Our Age of Anxiety is, in great part, the result of trying to do today's job with yesterday's tools.
> Marshall McLuhan
>
> Spoon feeding in the long run teaches us nothing but the shape of the spoon.
> E.M. Forster

In this chapter, we focus on several models or "tools" that we have found to be most useful in our work with students and with teachers. While there are certainly numerous other tools available, we believe that those we present here have stood the test of time and have proven to be "do-able" for most teachers. They also take full advantage of our current understandings of how learning occurs. What follows is only a brief introduction to each tool. We hope that you will seek to learn more about them, and other tools, as your students' needs dictate.

Tools for Differentiating Based on Student Readiness

When we work with teachers who are looking for ways to address a range of readiness levels in their classrooms, we often recommend that they consider using the following tools to guide them through lesson design: Bloom's Taxonomy, Tomlinson's Equalizer, and concept-based teaching.

Most teachers are familiar with **Bloom's Taxonomy** as it has been a staple of teacher education programs for over forty years. Originally designed as a means for identifying the degree of abstraction of questions that are typically asked in educational settings, this hierarchical model of thinking is now widely used to assist in the creation of assignments and tasks that address different levels of readiness. Whether using the original version of the Taxonomy or the newer one, it is important to keep the following truth in mind: Bloom did not intend for his model to be used as a means for labeling students. This means that we should not consider some students to generally be "knowledge-level" learners while others are "synthesis and evaluation" learners. Rather, we should keep in mind that

there are times when even our most struggling thinkers are capable of thinking at higher levels. Similarly, there are certainly times when our most gifted learners must focus on basic recall of information or "lower-level" thinking.

What makes Bloom's Taxonomy so appealing is that it can be applied to almost anything teachers create. Discussion questions, homework assignments, items for tests, and projects – all are possibilities. The trick in using this design structure, as with any instructional tool, is to make sure that students are being offered adequate and appropriate challenges. This means that we focus on students working at as high a level of thinking as possible given their readiness with regard to the content being studied.

Teachers must be careful to guard against "certain kinds of questions" for "certain kinds of students." It is reasonable to wonder, for example, if "lower-level" students are *never* asked to engage in "higher order" questions or exercises, when will they learn those higher-level thinking skills of synthesis and evaluation? Again, Bloom's Taxonomy was intended only to give teachers a *language for thinking* about their own instructional practices, **not** as a means for *classifying students*.

Tomlinson's Equalizer is a tool that asks teachers to consider how lessons and student work can be modified across nine separate dimensions. These dimensions include:

1. Foundational to transformational
2. Concrete to abstract
3. Simple to complex
4. Fewer facets to multi-facets
5. Smaller leap to greater leap
6. More structured to more open
7. Clearly-defined problems to fuzzy problems
8. Less independence to greater independence
9. Slower pace to quicker pace

(Carol Ann Tomlinson. The Differentiated Classroom: Responding to the Needs of All Learners. 1999.)

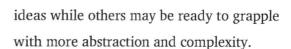

The greatest benefit of this tool is that it helps teachers think about ways to differentiate classroom learning across a wide range of student learning differences and needs. Rather than thinking in terms of "high ability" and "low ability," Tomlinson's Equalizer addresses characteristics of learners that might be related as much to their learning profiles as to their readiness. For example, we can certainly modify the amount of independence with which students are asked to work on a given assignment. We can also provide some students with a great deal of open-endedness in a given task while specifying for others a significantly greater degree of structure. In terms of readiness differences, some students may need to work with simpler, more concrete resources and ideas while others may be ready to grapple with more abstraction and complexity.

Tomlinson's Equalizer operates much like the knobs on a sound system's equalizer. By moving a knob from one end of the sound spectrum to the other, the sound quality of the music being produced can be modified to suit the listener's preferences. Likewise, a teacher using Tomlinson's Equalizer can move the knob anywhere along a given continuum to meet the needs of the students during any given lesson or with a particular task. Tomlinson's Equalizer reminds us that there are many ways to think about differences when it comes to student readiness and that there are many potential approaches we can consider as we respond to those differences.

Concept-based teaching directly addresses two of the dimensions on Tomlinson's *Equalizer*: concrete to abstract and simple to complex. When using this approach to instructional design, teachers focus on the larger ideas and the generalizations, or big statements, that can be made about those ideas. Concept-based teaching asks teachers to think about the "forest" rather than the "trees." For example, a unit on plants might become a study of *needs* and *environment* rather than simply a study of plant parts and how plants grow from seeds. What can be said about the needs of *any* living thing? Do those needs change depending on the *environment*? What is the relationship between a living organism's *needs* and its *environment*?

When we ask students to think about abstract ideas, or concepts, we require them to think at higher levels and encourage them to make connections across time and disciplines. Thus, the discussions held as part of the plant unit can be applied later to discussions of *community* and *jobs*. In addition to *needs* and e*nvironment*, some useful concepts that apply to many subject areas and topics at the elementary school level include (and this is just a short list of the many possibilities): change, patterns, exploration, communication, adaptation, systems, interdependence, power, survival, responsibility, courage, conflict, progress, growth, cycles, influence, and equality.

Tools for Differentiating Based on Student Learning Profiles

One of the easiest ways to address differing learning profiles in a classroom is to **provide variety in the environment and in the grouping arrangements**. What this means is that there are times when the room is silent, benefiting those who work best in silence, and there are other times when some noise is permitted, ben- efiting those who prefer some background sounds to do their best work. It also means that there are a variety of work spaces available to students, some of whom may need isolated or clean and organized work areas while others may be able to handle some nearby activity or clutter.

It is certainly the case that some of us do our best work on our own and prefer to work that way while others work best with a partner or in a group. In differentiated classrooms, teachers vary student groupings and often allow students to choose their own grouping configurations. Simply allowing students to work alone or with others when they want can mean the difference between a task that is finished only adequately and a job that is done well.

Another effective and frequently used tool for addressing learning profile differences is **Gardner's Multiple Intelligences**. Gardner originally conceived of seven different intelligences – verbal/linguistic, mathematical/logical, visual/spatial, musical, kinesthetic, interpersonal, and intrapersonal – and has since added an eighth and ninth, the naturalist and the spiritualist. With many publications supporting his theory, Gardner's model has become wildly popular in schools and is an effective and practical means for creating different tasks and product options. Certainly, it is a fairly simple one to understand and apply,

and by using it, a teacher is sure to be providing more variety in her teaching.

Our intent with this chapter was to revisit some lesson-design tools that teachers find useful when differentiating their instruction. There are thousands of teacher resources and web sites available that probe more deeply the rationale for and implementation of these tools and that discuss other possible tools as well. It is important to note that the models and approaches presented in this book are merely those that we have applied in the sample activities and tasks presented in Chapters 4 through 11. They also complement the specific strategies that are presented in Chapter 3.

Keep in mind that, regardless of the tools that a teacher chooses to use, the goal in any classroom, differentiated or not, ought to be to aim high so that each and every student experiences an appropriate challenge. Given the fact that our students enter our classrooms with vastly different needs and readiness levels for learning, aiming high for all cannot mean the same instruction and work for all. This is, of course, why differentiation is a necessity in any classroom.

Strategies for Differentiating Instruction

Variety is the spice of life.

- Unknown

It would be wonderful if one could go to a teacher supply store and simply purchase a kit for differentiating classroom instruction. Realistically, though, in any given classroom, that kit would not be tremendously responsive to students' needs, because it is really impossible for a teacher to predict ahead of time what needs might exist in a particular group. Differentiation is more of a philosophy and an approach to teaching than it is a collection of prescribed strategies. Therefore, it is up to individual teachers to decide just how differentiation will look and feel in their classrooms. It becomes each teacher's job to create his own "bag of tricks" for differentiating instruction.

> It is a fundamental truth that children need well-educated teachers who are eclectic in their methods and willing to use different strategies, depending on what works best for which children.
>
> Diane Ravitch,
> Left Back: A Century of
> Failed School Reforms
> (2000)

We have been delivering workshops and in-service sessions on the concept and practice of differentiation for years. After the many hours of discussing, modeling, and practicing differentiation with a particular group of teachers, one central observation always remains true: each and every teacher leaves our time together with a different plan of action and with different goals for differentiating. If each of those teachers has sat through the same workshop session, how can it be that there are so many diverse outcomes? The answer is simple: not every teacher's needs are the same; not every teacher's comfort level with the concepts presented is the same; not every teacher's support system back in the school building is the same. In short, none of our workshop participants are the same. What they pick and choose to use after working with us necessarily differs.

This being said, we have chosen to focus on three strategies that *most* elementary teachers find useful – tiered assignments, RAFT activities, and Think-Tac-Toes. Typically, teachers ask to see more examples of these particular strategies for use in their own classrooms. It may be helpful to flip to some of the examples provided in the sub- ject area chapters as you read about each of these strategies in the passages below. We recognize that we could have included many more strategies, and we hope that you will continue your own search to learn more about strategies that support differentiation (See the *Resources* provided at the end of the book).

Tiered Assignments

Also known as "tiering" or "tiered in-struction," tiered assignments are often the first strategy that teachers learn about as they begin their work with differentiation. It is difficult to imagine a differentiated class-room that does not at some point include tiered assignments. In fact, teachers who are unfamiliar with differentiation are often un-der the mistaken impression that tiered as-signments are all there is to it.

Tiered assignments are based on student readiness and result in students either work-ing together in small groups, in pairs, or in-dividually to complete tasks that are based on their readiness levels. This means that teachers using tiered assignments first iden-tify the objectives that they need to teach and then find a way to assess students' cur-rent grasp of those objectives. Whether from their prior experiences teaching specif-ic content or from formal and informal assessment measures, teachers know their students do not all grasp and under-stand the

> Tiered assignments are based on student readi-ness and result in stu-dents either working together in small groups, in pairs, or in-dividually to complete tasks that are based on their readiness levels.

same amount of material in the same way at the same rate. Good teachers intuitively rec-ognize that students have developed differ-ent skill sets, either in school or out, and that their students are at different points in terms of conceptual development. Once teachers recognize that these kinds of differences in readiness exist in their classrooms, tiered assignments become a necessity and a convenient way to address this issue.

We tend to think in terms of three groups or three different assignments when tiering: an assignment for students who are lacking a good deal of prior knowledge and experience with regard to the objectives; an assignment for students who have mastered all of the objectives (or can do so quickly); and an assignment for those who fall somewhere in between. There are certainly times, though, when two tiers is sufficient for meeting students' needs, and there may even be times when a particular group of students requires more than three tiers.

It is tempting to put students into groups that ultimately remain fairly static. However, teachers in differentiated classrooms recognize that a student's readiness can change, sometimes very rapidly. One day a student can be lagging behind with regard to specific content or objectives, but the next day that same student might be ready to make a leap of some sort. At the elementary school level, it can be dangerous to underestimate the role of home life, personal experience, and social issues in the readiness of students, and the changing nature of the content from unit to unit within a subject area certainly has an impact on student readiness. For these reasons, teachers in differentiated classrooms must adopt a flexible approach to assigning tasks to students. They understand that on any given day they may have to rethink the assignment they have planned for a particular student or group of students.

Because tiered assignments are based on student readiness and result in different levels of activities, teachers choose which assignment each student will complete. It would be nice if each student in a third-grade classroom, for example, would select the option that is appropriately challenging for her. But as all teachers know, students do not always make the best choices, and many will seek the "easy" way out. There are many times in a differentiated classroom when students ought to be given choices. It is just not wise to give them those choices when differentiating based on readiness.

Typically, teachers go through the following steps when tiering an assignment or activity.

1) **Identify the objectives to be tiered.** It is important to keep in mind that if the objectives are those that all students have already mastered, then there is no reason to teach them again directly. If they are objectives that no students in a class have mastered, then standard whole group instruction may be preferable, making tiering unnecessary.

2) **Pre-assess students' grasp of the objectives.** Pre-assessment can take many forms, formal or informal. The trick is to make sure that your pre-assessment is clearly aligned with your objectives. An assessment is of little use if it does not tell us what we need to know about a student's knowledge, understanding, and skill level.

3) **Design or find one activity that addresses the objectives.** This activity is the basis for the other "tiers," so it should be a good one. This means that it should clearly address the objectives, that it should be age-appropriate and respectful of students' abilities, and that it should be engaging. It is a good idea to aim to the middle or high groups when developing this first activity as this will help ensure that your expectations for all your tiers will be high. Remember, the middle group represents the more typical students who are neither the "slowest" nor the "brightest." Starting the planning process with the lowest tier in mind often results in low expectations for all tiers.

4) **Design or find other tiers as needed.** As mentioned previously, there is no rule about the number of tiers a teacher should provide. Some content and classes might require only two tiers while others may occasionally require four or perhaps even five. If you are just starting to differentiate, we recommend beginning with fewer tiers and working your way up to more as needed. If you move beyond three groups, a central question you might consider before you begin planning those additional activities is, "What, *really*, is the key difference between the needs of Group Four and Group Five?" If you can delineate these unique needs, then moving forward with further tiered assignments is appropriate.

5) **Assign students to the appropriate tiered assignment.** At this point, it helps to have spent some time analyzing the students' pre-assessments to determine which assignments will provide both challenge and success to which students. Are there some students who "aced" the pre-assessment while others struggled to complete most of the items on it? Which items are students missing? Time spent reflecting on the students' prior knowledge will help enormously when it is time to decide who does which tiered assignment. When it comes to actually giving the appropriate assignments to students, we do not advise discussing all of the assignments with the whole class. This draws unnecessary attention to the fact that students will be completing different tasks. It is a better idea to give students only the assignments that they will be responsible for completing.

6) **Be ready to make changes.** There is no accounting for changes, sometimes rapid, in students' readiness for learning, so it is a good idea to be flexible when assigning tiered activities. But guess what? The same is true for you as well! Remember, even moving from a standard practice of whole group instruction to an assignment that includes two tiers represents progress on your part. Your goal should not be to change your instructional practices en masse. Start small, experience some success, evaluate the difficulties, and always try, try again.

Tiered assignments are ultimately the backbone of the differentiated classroom. They allow teachers to respond to the fact that some students enter our classrooms with vast amounts of prior knowledge while others are sorely lacking in information and skills. And yet, we need to find a way to challenge them all.

RAFT Activities

RAFT activities can be great fun to design and complete. Once teachers learn about this strategy, they often find themselves using it again and again. RAFT is an acronym for **R**OLE, **A**UDIENCE, **F**ORMAT, and **T**OPIC. When designing these activities, teachers must consider the roles they want their students to assume, the audiences that students should address, the formats (most often written) that students' work can take, and the topics to which students must respond. As with tiered assignments, when designing RAFT activities, teachers should first be clear about their unit's objectives.

The great thing about RAFT activities is that they allow for a great deal of creativity for both teachers and students while providing many avenues for differentiation. A teacher might want to address student readiness differences by differentiating the abstractness of the role students will take on or the complexity of the topic they will address. On the other hand, she might choose to respond to learning profile differences in her classroom by coming up with a variety of different formats for students' products. For example, a letter or speech draws on verbal/linguistic intelligence while a top-ten list or time line draws on mathematical/logical skills. RAFT assignments are a multi-faceted strategy in that they can also be used as part of other strategies for differentiation. For example, RAFT assignments can be used as tiered assignments and as options on Think-Tac-Toes.

RAFT activities can be used in all subject areas and at all grade levels to encourage students to apply and analyze information and understandings that they have mastered or are mastering. And these activities can be either teacher-assigned or student-selected, depending on how they are differentiated.

It is important to keep in mind that when RAFT activities are differentiated based on student readiness they should be assigned by the teacher. However, students can certainly be allowed to choose the activity they want to work on when the activities have been differentiated based on some other criteria, such as student learning profile or interest. Probably the most difficult part of creating effective RAFT activities is ensuring that they are linked to previously-identified objectives. However, this challenge is outweighed by the fact that teachers often enjoy creating these highly-engaging activities.

> The great thing about RAFT activities is that they allow for a great deal of creativity for both teachers and students while providing many avenues for differentiation.

Think-Tac-Toes

Of all the strategies we share with teachers, Think-Tac-Toes usually spark the greatest interest. While tiered assignments are fundamental to a differentiated classroom and allow for a great deal of "teacher control," many teachers seem most drawn to Think-Tac-Toes. And students like them, too, because they provide a great deal of choice. Think-Tac-Toes are in essence a form of learning contracts. When designed well, they invite students to work in ways that are based on their learning profiles and interests and that focus on important knowledge, understandings, and skills. They make very effective assessments at the end of a unit, and teachers often use them in addition to more formal assessments.

Typically, Think-Tac-Toes are created in three by three grids, providing nine possible tasks. Students select a given number of tasks to complete, but three tasks is generally the goal. It is up to the teacher to decide if students need to connect the tasks in rows, columns, or diagonally. A great way to "tighten up" a Think-Tac-Toe is to make each row focus on a particular objective or aspect of the content and then ask students to choose one task from each row.

Because students make choices based on their learning profiles and interests in the tasks to be completed on a Think-Tac-Toe, it is critical to keep the readiness levels of the tasks fairly similar. If students discover that some tasks are simpler than others, they may choose those tasks and avoid the more challenging items that might in fact be more appropriate for them. Teachers aiming to address readiness while using Think-Tac-Toes should be prepared to tier them, thus creating two or more Think-Tac-Toes and then assigning the appropriate tiered Think-Tac-Toe grids to the students needing them (see the *Tiered Literature Think-Tac-Toes* provided in Chapter 8). This practice allows the teacher to provide students with choice while ensuring that they are being adequately challenged. As with any strategy for differentiation, it is important to maintain focus on the objectives – something that can be difficult to do during the process of creating a variety of tasks.

> Think-Tac-Toes make very effective assessments at the end of a unit, and teachers often use them in addition to more formal assessments.

Some Final Thoughts

Some strategies for differentiating instruction take longer to plan and prepare than others. For instance, RAFT activities can be fairly simple to create because there is a prescribed format for doing so, while creating Think-Tac-Toes tends to take much more effort and time. It is typical, though, for students to spend a longer amount of time working on Think-Tac-Toe tasks than on RAFT activities so the "teacher planning time" to "student work time" ratio is fairly equal. And while it might take some time to create tiered projects, designing tiered writing prompts may take much less time. Again, differentiated instruction will look different in every classroom in which it is implemented.

Effective classroom management is crucial in any classroom, but it takes on even more importance in a differentiated classroom where students are often expected to take responsibility for their own learning. It is easy to understate the need for the practice of routines in a differentiated classroom, but that practice is often the difference between a classroom where differentiation runs smoothly and one where it does not.

Students must be able to move effectively and efficiently from one place in the classroom to another (a kitchen timer and serious consequences work wonders with this). They need to know where finished work goes, where unfinished work goes, and where to find the materials necessary for task completion.

Another important management consideration focuses on keeping students engaged, even when the teacher is not working directly with them or when they are not sure what they should be doing at a particular moment. There are times in all classrooms, for instance, when students finish work and assessments early or come to a point in their work where they can go no further without assistance from the teacher. Teachers in differentiated classrooms use **anchor activities** to ensure that student engagement continues despite these issues.

Anchor activities are tasks that students can do and will do on their own. Silent reading can be a great anchor activity, but only for those students who enjoy reading. For those who do not, it can be an enormous chore, perhaps even a punishment, and is not likely to keep them engaged. Many teachers post a list of possible anchor activities so that students have some choice in the tasks they will complete on their own. Effective anchor activities focus on important skills and are not busywork. They can relate to a specific unit or they can be more generic. Examples of anchor activities include: independent projects, puzzles and games, journaling, creative thinking tasks and activities, and computer programs. Again, it is important to find and create **anchor activities that focus on essential skills.**

Anchor activities can also ease the difficulties associated with assigning different work to different students. Having these sorts of activities ready is useful when a teacher needs to present a task to one group before interacting with other groups. While she works with one

> When students understand why differentiation is necessary and that the classroom can be responsive to them, they are much more likely to take responsibility for making the classroom routines successful.

group to get them started on their assignment, the rest of the students can be engaged with anchor activities.

As a final note, keep in mind that no amount of training will make differentiation easier if the students do not buy into the idea of it. For this reason, teachers and students in differentiated classrooms spend a good deal of time discussing the need for differentiation. When students understand why differentiation is necessary and that the classroom can be responsive to them, they are much more likely to take responsibility for making the classroom routines successful.

Readiness-Based Language Arts Tiered Assignments

Composing Well-Structured Paragraphs

<u>Overview</u>: *These tiered activities provide a scaffolded approach to the tricky skill of composing paragraphs that feature a solid focus, beginning with attention to a thoughtful topic sentence and including supporting details that appeal to more than one of the reader's senses.*

Standard:
➢ Plan and make judgments about what to include in written products (e.g., narratives of personal experiences, creative stories, skits based on familiar stories and/or experiences)

Objectives:

The students will **KNOW**
- The parts of a paragraph.
- The definition of a *topic sentence.*

The students will **UNDERSTAND THAT**
- A well-structured paragraph contains definite and discernible elements, including a topic sentence and supporting details.
- A topic sentence expresses a subject *and* some opinion on that subject.
- Sufficient and focused elaboration on a topic is essential to educating a reader about that topic.
- Well-written paragraphs contain a logical structure that assists the reader in comprehending and examining an author's opinion about a given topic.
- An author's structural decisions and word choice can dramatically affect a reader's ability to comprehend a piece of writing.

The students will **BE ABLE TO**
- Recognize and apply standard text formatting in the composition of a paragraph.
- Compose first drafts using an appropriate writing process which includes:
  ❖ Planning and drafting.
  ❖ Rereading for meaning.
  ❖ Revising to clarify and refine writing with guided discussion.

Materials:
- For Tier One (lower readiness): Copies of the worksheet below and on page 29-30, scissors
- For Tier Two (middle readiness): Copies of the worksheet on page 31, selection of assorted magazines
- For Tier Three (higher readiness): Copies of the assignment on page 33, a collection of unusual objects, markers, poster board

Tier One (lower readiness)

Part One: Your teacher will assign you one of the following boxed exercises. Begin by cutting the sentences apart. Then arrange them into a well-structured paragraph. Once you have done this, with a partner share your paragraphs to see if they make sense. Which paragraph makes more sense? Why? Be sure to identify the topic sentence first and then find all of the supporting details.

When he was in first grade he already knew all of his multiplication tables up to the twelves.
Of all the students in Sherwood Elementary, Scott was definitely the smartest.
He wrote a book when he was in fourth grade, and he won the international chess championships in fifth grade.
There's no telling what he'll do when he gets to middle school!
By the end of second grade, he had won the national spelling bee.
In third grade, he helped his teacher plan all the science lessons so she could teach them to the rest of the class.

Usually, you get to stay up a little later than normal because the trick-or-treating doesn't start until after dark.

The best part is that it's the one time of year when you can gets lots of candy – for free!

While you're walking around, you can look at all the other people who are out trick-or-treating and try to guess who they are.

Halloween is my favorite of all the holidays.

I only wish Halloween came more than one time a year!

I like it because you get to dress up like anything you want to be – from an astronaut to a zoo keeper.

Every morning it gets up and barks at the top of its lungs before the roosters rise.

I wouldn't think about entering that dog in any dog shows soon!

It bares its teeth, hangs its tongue out, and slobbers lavishly.

When it growls, it sounds like an angry cat.

My neighbor's dog is one of the strangest pets I've ever seen.

It runs at top speed around the yard, digging holes and tearing azaleas from the ground.

His short hair makes him look weird too.

Part Two: Now, with a partner, complete the following activity. Read the topic sentences below. Choose one. Create three supporting detail sentences to illustrate your chosen topic sentence.

Example: The Tyrannosaurus Rex was one of the fiercest dinosaurs.

- Its sharp teeth were eight inches long and were sharp enough to cut meat to the bone.
- It was so tall that it towered over most other dinosaurs.
- Its powerful legs allowed it to run at top speed when it chased its prey.

❖ _____ is the best/worst show on television.
  Name of a television show

  -

  -

  -

❖ _____ is my favorite/least favorite class in school.
  Name of a school subject

  -

  -

  -

❖ _____ is the most exciting experience I've ever had.
  Something you've done

  -

  -

  -

Tier Two (middle readiness)

Warm-Up Activity One: Do on your own.

Charles wrote a paper about his family reunion this past summer. Below are some selected sentences from that essay. Choose three (3), and turn them into sentences that express the idea more specifically. Be creative!

Example: The hotel we stayed in was shabby. ——▶ The hotel room we stayed in had a leaky bathroom shower faucet and its tattered carpet needed to be replaced.

It was hard to get there.	It was hot outside.
The meal tasted great.	My sister was grumpy.
My uncle's dog looked like it was crazy.	I was bored.
My aunt is nice.	Dad talked a lot.
I have a lot of cousins.	Grandpa dresses oddly.

Activity Two: Your teacher will give you and a partner a magazine. Look carefully at the pictures inside, and note their details. Select one picture, and brainstorm a great topic sentence based on something you see in that picture. Remember, a topic sentence not only states what the topic is, but it also expresses some kind of opinion about that topic! Finally, brainstorm and write at least four (4) good detail sentences that help prove or illustrate your topic sentence's observation.

For example, if your teacher handed you a bridal magazine, you might write the following.

Topic Sentence:

The bride in this picture is very nervous about her wedding day.

Note that this sentence features a *topic* (the bride) and it expresses an *opinion* about that topic (she is nervous).

The topic sentence was *not* just: *A lady is getting married.*

Supporting details: She is frowning as she looks at her dress in the mirror.

She seems to be yelling at someone on her cell phone.

The tailor trying to help her seems a little scared of her.

Her hair is messed up, like she's been running her hands through it often.

Activity Three: Now, do Activity Two again, but this time, do it alone choosing a different picture. Write your topic sentence and supporting detail sentences in the form of a real, bona-fide paragraph. Remember to indent and use complete sentences!

Tier Three (higher readiness)

Your teacher will give you and your partner a small collection of unusual objects. Your task is the following:

First, examine the assorted items and choose one.

Second, brainstorm a list of all the uses your object might have. Be creative!

Third, create a magazine advertisement that illustrates your object's purpose and sells it to an audience.

Here are the specific requirements for your ad:

✓ A clever topic sentence should express the object's purpose in some enthusiastic way.

✓ You should provide plenty of reasons to explain how revolutionary this product is.

✓ Your ad should use lots of imagery, including at least one simile or metaphor.

✓ Remember, although it is an ad, you should still follow the conventions of proper English. Pay attention to spelling, capitalization, and punctuation.

✓ Do not wander off topic!

Your teacher may ask you to present this to the rest of the class, so be ready!

Closure: When the students have finished their assigned tasks, have the students share their individual understandings about the following elements of a well-structured paragraph:

The role of the topic sentence:
- It expresses a topic plus some specific opinion about that topic.
- It can be illustrated with many different examples or details.

The role of supporting details:
- They should all work to help illustrate the topic sentence.
- They should not stray from the topic sentence.
- They can be expressed in a variety of creative ways and should appeal to the reader's various senses.

Show a paragraph that is not well structured on the overhead, and ask the students to share ways to improve it.

Compound Words

Overview: ***Students will complete these tiered products after an introduction to and practice with compound words.*** Prior to assigning these products, use the following types of activities both to familiarize students with compound words and to assess their understanding of and skill with them. Thus, as students engage in these introductory and skill-building activities, the teacher's task is to observe and interact with students in order to assign them to the appropriate tiered product based on their readiness levels.

❖ Use a concept attainment activity to introduce compound words. In this type of activity, a teacher shares a list of words that are compound words (the "IN" list) along with a list of words that are not compound words (the "OUT" list). Students are invited to add words to either list and to discover what it takes to be included on the "IN" list.

❖ Read books about compound words (for example, All Aboard Overnight: A Book of Compound Words by Betsy Maestro and Giulio Maestro and Once There Was a Bull-Frog by Rick Walton).

❖ Create a class list of compound words and post for all to see.

❖ Create compound words using "banks" of words provided on worksheets or on word cards. This activity can be differentiated by having lower-readiness students create compound words that have already been discussed while higher-readiness students create "new" compound words and/or use compound words in sentences.

Standard:
➢ Use a variety of word identification strategies to read and write
Objectives:
The students will **KNOW**
• The definition of *compound word.*
• Examples of compound words.
The students will **UNDERSTAND THAT**
• Some words can be combined to create larger, compound words.

The students will **BE ABLE TO**
- Use cues to recognize compound words.
- Read, spell, and write compound words.
- Use resources to find correct spellings.

Materials:
- Copies of *A Superday at the Ball Park* for students working at Tier Three

Tier One (lower readiness)

Students working at this tier create illustrated books of compound words. They may work with others at this tier to brainstorm compound words, but each student creates his or her own book. Each page in the book must show a compound word as well as a picture that illustrates that word. If they are able to do so, students can also create a sentence to go along with each compound word.

Tier Two (middle readiness)

Students assigned to this tier work independently to create a story, song, or poem that includes at least 8 compound words. They may work with others assigned to this tier to brainstorm compound words, but each student must create his or her own product.

Tier Three (higher readiness)

Students at this tier act as "compound detectives" as they read through the following story to locate "rogue" compound words. Using dictionaries as needed and as the students are able, they look for words that are written as compound words but should not be. They also look for words that are *not* written as compound words but should be. The students circle the mistakes they find and correct them on a separate piece of paper. Time permitting, the students create their own stories with "rogue" compound words and share them with others working at this tier.

A Superday at the Ball Park

Sabrina and Marcus visited the ball park on Saturday to see a base ball game.

They cheered for their team, the Bulls, and ate until their stomachs hurt. Sabrina loved

the cottoncandy, while Marcus filled up on hot dogs and frenchfries. The most exciting

moment in the ball game came when the Bulls' starplayer hit a long home run. The score

board lit up and the crowd roared! During the eighth inning, the sun began to set, and

Sabrina and Marcus knew it was close to their bed time. So, they packed up their souve-

nirs and headed home. That night, Sabrina dreamed of batters hitting home runs, while

Marcus dreamed of foot ball!

Closure: Allow students to share their products with one another. To save time, they can do this in mixed-readiness, small groups so that they have an opportunity to see the products that other students completed.

For a whole-group closure activity, write a word, such as *sun* or *ball*, on the board, and ask the students to brainstorm compound words that include that word.

Consonants and Vowels

Overview: *These activities give students independent practice with distinguishing consonants and vowels and should follow an introduction to and some practice with identifying them*. For example, while reciting the alphabet, students can stand up or raise their hands every time they come to a vowel. In addition, make available alphabet posters, sets of manipulative letters, or index cards with letters that show consonants and vowels in different colors.

Standard:
  ➢ Develop and apply strategies to read and write

Objectives:
The students will **KNOW**
   • Letters that are consonants.
   • Letters that are vowels.
The students will **UNDERSTAND THAT**
   • The alphabet is made up of consonants and vowels.
   • Words are made up of letters that have sounds.
The students will **BE ABLE TO**
   • Identify letters of the alphabet.
   • Distinguish between consonants and vowels.

Materials:
  • "Color by letter" page (These can be found in phonetics/alphabet workbooks or they can be made by the teacher.)
  • Crayons or colored pencils
  • Word splash including some words that begin with consonants and others that begin with vowels (A word splash is a collection of words that are randomly placed on a page and that may or may not have something in common.)

Tier One (lower readiness)

Students working at this tier, most likely students who are not reading and may need some support with letter recognition, use two colors to complete a "color by letter" page. They should color all spaces that show a consonant using one of the colors. The spaces showing vowels should be colored the second color. When they have completed their coloring, the students should see a picture of something familiar to them.

Tier Two (higher readiness)

Students working at this tier circle words on a word splash that start with vowels. When they have finished, they may either add more words that begin with vowels or create another word splash for a classmate to complete.

Closure: Working with the whole group, write simple, one-syllable words on the board, read them to the students, and ask the students to identify the consonants and vowels in the words. In addition, show how changing the vowel in a word, but not the consonants, changes the whole word. For instance:

RAG ⇔ RUG   TIN ⇔ TAN

Pose a question such as:
How many words can we make with the consonants H and T? (H__T)
Use other possibilities as needed.

Exploring a Concept (Survival) Through Literature

Overview: *These tiered activities demonstrate that students can explore at different levels of complexity and abstractness the concepts or "big ideas" that are highlighted in the novels that they read.* This particular set of tasks addresses the concept of *survival*, a concept highlighted by novels such as The Green Book, The Swiss Family Robinson, and many others. Students' work with concepts addressed in literature gives teachers ample assessment data regarding students' reading comprehension, their grasp of larger understandings related to both literature and life, and their ability to make connections. Thus, these tasks can be an informative part of the summative evaluation for a novel or literature study. These particular activities also make good "hooks" to begin a novel study.

Standard:
➢ Connect, compare, and contrast ideas, themes, and issues across texts and with real life

Objectives:
The students will **KNOW**
- The definition of *survival*.

The students will **UNDERSTAND THAT**
These statements should be discussed with students prior to their beginning work on the tasks outlined below.
- All living things want to survive.
- Sometimes we have to adapt to survive.
- We survive when our basic needs are met.
- We can survive without having everything we want.

The students will **BE ABLE TO**
- Make decisions to impact survival.
- Evaluate items in terms of their necessity to survival.

Materials:
- *What Would You Choose?* page 42
- Blank index cards
- The following terms written on index cards (one set for each group working on the Tier Two assignment): *food, friendship, love, water, books, music, basketball, fire, TV*

Tier One (lower readiness)

Students assigned to this tier will work either independently or in pairs.

Using the sheet *What Would You Choose?*, brainstorm no more than seven items that you would want to have if you were stranded alone in the woods. Then, explain why you would want each item.

Tier Two (middle readiness)

Students assigned to this tier will work in small groups of no more than four students per group.

Work as a group to brainstorm at least eight items that you use on a daily basis. Write each of these items on an index card. Combine your cards with the cards provided that show the following: *food, friendship, love, water, books, music, basketball, fire, TV*. Your task is to decide as a group how important each item is to survival. To do so, your group will place the cards in order from *Not at All Important* to *Highly Important*. When you have the cards in an order that you can all agree on, work together to write a paragraph about the order you have decided on. Questions to consider include:

✓ Which item is most important to survival? Why?

✓ Which item is least important? Why?

✓ What general statement(s) can you make about items that are important to survival?

Tier Three (higher readiness)

Students assigned to this tier will work in pairs.

You have found yourselves in the desert, penniless, homeless, and alone. Create a plan for how you will survive for one week. How will you get food, drink, shelter, and clothing? How will you work together to survive? Find a detailed, creative, and neat way to show your work.

Closure: Pose the following questions to the whole group:
- Would you want to be on the TV show Survivor? Why or why not?
- If you knew you were going to travel somewhere unknown and might not return home, what items would you want to have with you? Why?
- What if all your needs were already provided for?
- What if you could only bring two items?
- What if one of the items had to be a book? Which book would you choose? Why?

What Would You Choose?

SOS! You are stranded alone in the woods far from civilization and all that you know. What would you most like to have with you right now? You have no idea when, or IF, you will be rescued or will be able to find your way out of the woods. What items would you want and WHY? Here are your requirements:

- ☐ All items should be small enough to fit in your pocket.
- ☐ You are limited to a maximum of 7 items.
- ☐ You may not include any communications devices in your list.

Use this table to list your items, and record your reasons for wanting them.

Item	Reason for wanting it

Folktale Motifs

Overview: *These tiered tasks should follow extensive reading of a variety of folktales. Once students have listened to, read, and discussed several folktales, they should be ready to look at some motifs, or patterns, present in almost all folktales.* These tasks focus on five major motifs: magical powers, transformations, magic objects, wishes, and trickery. Some folktales that address these motifs include:

❖ Magical powers: <u>Rumpelstiltskin</u>, <u>Moss Gown</u>, <u>The Seven Chinese Brothers</u>

❖ Transformations: <u>Beauty and the Beast</u>, <u>The Princess and the Frog</u>, <u>The Crane Wife</u>, <u>Cinderella</u>

❖ Magic objects: <u>Aladdin</u>, <u>Strega Nona</u>, <u>The Talking Eggs</u>, <u>Jack and the Beanstalk</u>

❖ Wishes: <u>The Three Wishes</u>, <u>Momotaro, the Peach Boy</u>, <u>The Fisherman and His Wife</u>

❖ Trickery: <u>Stone Soup</u>, <u>The Boy of the Three Year Nap</u>, <u>Lon Po Po</u>

Before the students working at the lower tier begin their assigned tasks, they should meet with the teacher to discuss these five motifs. Students working at the higher tier should not hear this discussion.

Standards:
➢ Recognize the characteristics of various types of texts
➢ Recognize the distinguishing features of familiar genres
➢ Connect ideas and themes across texts

Objectives:
The students will **KNOW**
• The titles of a variety of folktales.
• The basic characteristics of folktales (for example, quick introduction and action, repetition, one-dimensional characters: good guys versus bad guys).

The students will **UNDERSTAND THAT**
• Different literary genres have different characteristics.
• Folktales are stories that have been "handed down" over time.
• The types, characteristics, and motifs of folktales can help us to compare and contrast different folktales.

The students will **BE ABLE TO**
• Identify motifs in folktales.
• Categorize examples of motifs.
• Work cooperatively.

Materials:
- A variety of folktales (multiple copies, if possible)
- Index cards showing the five motifs (enough sets for several small groups)
- Index cards showing many examples of motifs from a range of folktales (enough sets for several small groups)

Closure: As a whole group, the students share their work. Students assigned to the first tier share which stories best illustrate the motifs they worked with. Students who worked at the second tier share the motif categories that they created. Do they match the categories that the other students worked with? Other discussion questions include:
- Can you think of any other folktale motifs?
- In what folktales do you see these motifs?
- Which is your favorite folktale motif? Why?

Tier One (lower readiness)

Students at this tier work in small groups to brainstorm examples of magical powers, transformations, magic objects, wishes, and trickery (written on separate index cards) present in the folktales that they have listened to and/or read. They draw and label the examples they generate on five sheets of paper, each representing a different motif. Have them label each sheet with the name of the motif illustrated on it.

The groups then select one story for each motif that best illustrates the use of that particular motif. For example, which folktale includes the best example of a transformation? The groups should be able to explain their choices.

Tier Two (higher readiness)

Students assigned to this tier work in small groups to categorize examples of motifs without knowing the names of the motifs. Given many motif examples on index cards (for example, *magic beans* and *becoming a handsome prince*), they create groups for the examples and name these groups. How can the examples be grouped? Why? Challenge the student groups to change their motif categories. Are there other ways to group the examples? What is the best way to group them?

Once the students have agreed on a particular way to group the examples, they should be ready to explain their categories.

Handwriting Center

Overview: *Because students bring a wide range of writing abilities to primary classrooms, teachers need to be ready to respond to differences in the area of writing.* Centers provide time and space for students to work on skills at their own paces and readiness levels and, thus, are an effective means of addressing student differences. These handwriting center activities engage students while allowing them to begin at their individual starting points and then grow at rates that match their expanding abilities in handwriting. Take time to introduce these activities as students are ready for them and observe students' work with the activities so they can help students move through the different tiers as they are ready.

Standards:
  ➤ Develop the foundations of writing
  ➤ Gain increasing control of penmanship

Objectives:
The students will **KNOW**
  • The letters of the alphabet.
The students will **UNDERSTAND THAT**
  • Print represents spoken language and conveys meaning.
  • Basic skills improve with practice.
The students will **BE ABLE TO**
  • Write each letter of the alphabet in both upper and lower case.
  • Write his or her name.
  • Copy text.
  • Write messages that move top to bottom and left to right.
  • Write to record ideas and reflections.
  • Use word and letter spacing to make writing readable.

Materials:
  • Poster showing desired formation of upper and lower case letters (posted for all to see)
  • Small, laminated copies of the alphabet showing desired letter formation (for individual student use)
  • Small trays (for sand writing, Styrofoam vegetable trays work well)
  • Sand (preferably colored)
  • Index cards showing students' names
  • Copies of strips of paper showing individual letters and space to practice writing them (to save time and paper, these can be laminated for reuse with dry-erase markers)

- Copies of writing paper showing words to be copied (to save time and paper, these can be laminated for reuse with dry-erase markers)
- Copies of writing paper showing poems and riddles to be copied
- Blank writing paper
- Index cards showing writing activities

Handwriting Center Activities

The following activities are listed in order of difficulty beginning with the least difficult tasks. Match the students' starting points along the continuum of activities with the students' current handwriting abilities. Thus, a student who is struggling to write individual letters might begin with sand writing, while a student who has mastered letter formation and can write his or her own name might begin with copying words and poems. Some students may be able to write their own names but may not be able to write letters that are not included in their names. Thus, it may be necessary for some students to practice letters not included in their names.

Sand writing

Using a copy of the alphabet as a guide, students will practice writing letters in sand.

Task #2

Practice with specific letters

Students will practice writing individual letters on strips of paper that show models of the letters. Encourage students to practice letters that are difficult for them (the teacher can provide students with individualized lists of letters to be practiced).

Task #3

Practice with writing their own names

Using index cards showing their names, students will practice writing their own names correctly.

Task #4

Copying words

Students will practice writing on writing paper complete words that are provided. Words to be copied can include numbers one through ten, colors, and weather words.

Task #5

Copying poems and riddles

Students will practice writing on writing paper poems and riddles that are provided. The works of Jack Prelutsky and Shel Silverstein provide many examples of short poems and riddles that students will enjoy writing on their own.

Task #6

Writing activity cards

Students will select and complete writing activities provided on index cards. These activities can be stored in a small box and can include the following:

- ✓ Write a poem about a special time of year
- ✓ Write a poem about anything you want
- ✓ Find and copy a poem that you like
- ✓ Write a letter to a friend
- ✓ Write a letter to a pet
- ✓ Write a letter to a parent telling about your school day
- ✓ Write a letter to a family member telling about things you like to do
- ✓ Write sentences about yourself
- ✓ Write about your family
- ✓ Write about your favorite holiday
- ✓ Write about your favorite place
- ✓ Write about your favorite animal
- ✓ Write about a place you would like to visit
- ✓ List 10 foods that you like to eat
- ✓ Write sentences telling how to do something that you like to do
- ✓ Write sentences about your pet
- ✓ Write sentences about your favorite cartoon character
- ✓ Write sentences about your favorite story
- ✓ Write sentences about your favorite sports team
- ✓ Write sentences about your favorite movie
- ✓ Make up and write an original story

Mechanics
(Apostrophes, Capitalization, and Commas)

Overview: *Because students bring a wide range of writing abilities to the elementary classroom, it is important for teachers to be ready to respond to these differences in the area of mechanics.* These tasks provide opportunities for students to work on three specific skills at their own levels of readiness and, thus, are an effective means of addressing student discrepancies regarding the command of essential written mechanics.

Standard:
> ➢ Demonstrate a command of essential punctuation and mechanics to create a variety of descriptive sentences

Objectives:

The students will **KNOW**
- The function of a given punctuation mark in a sentence, specifically commas (and their differences from periods) and apostrophes.
- The reasons for capitalizing some words in a given sentence.

The students will **UNDERSTAND THAT**
- Punctuation marks and capitalization help convey specific types of meaning in a piece of writing.
- Punctuation and capitalization help to guide the reader in decoding complex and compound sentences.

The students will **BE ABLE TO**
- Correctly apply punctuation rules to a given sentence.
- Correctly apply punctuation rules to a given sentence to delineate a sentence's descriptive phrases and clauses.
- Correctly apply capitalization rules to given words.

Materials:
- Paper, pencils
- Sets of dice of differing colors, alphabet cards
- Magazines or newspapers
- Printed sheets showing the activities described below
- Printed copies of the teacher's selected essential mechanic rules

Explanation of the Activities

The following activities within each topic are listed in order of difficulty beginning with the least difficult tasks. It is assumed that the highest level tier is composed of students who thoroughly understand the objective. Match the students' starting points along the continuum of activities with the students' current grasp of the various mechanics and punctuation topics. Furthermore, it must be made clear that the rules, at least as they have been numbered and arranged in this tiered lesson, are fairly arbitrary. Rearrange, renumber, add, or even delete rules according to individual state curricular and classroom differentiation needs. The rules provided here are simply intended to be a model for the lesson design and implementation.

Apostrophe Rules (for expressing ownership)

Rule #1: When showing ownership with a word that is *singular*, you may always add **'s**.

- The cover of the book → the book's cover   The arm of the boy → the boy's arm

Rule #2: If the word is singular and ends with **s**, you may simply add just the apostrophe.

- The pen of the boss → the boss' pen   The rim of the glass → the glass' rim

Rule #3: When showing ownership of *plural* nouns that end in **s**, add only the apostrophe.

- The windows of the cars → the cars' windows   The names of the guys → the guys' names

Rule #4: When showing ownership of plural nouns that do **not** end in **s**, add **'s**.

- The ideas of the men → the men's ideas   The antlers of the deer → the deer's antlers

Picture Sort

Given a wide variety of pictures (from magazines, newspapers, clipart, etc.), the students:

1. Write what the picture represents to them. For example, this is to help distinguish between a "mug" versus a "glass."
2. Sort the words/pictures into four categories according to the rule categories above. For example, a picture of a "car" would go into the sort for Rule #1, but a picture of "geese" would go into the sort for Rule #4.
3. Select two from each category and create descriptive sentences that use the rule in context. For example: *I really like the cars' bright colors.*

Standard Sentence Correction

Students practice correcting given sentences that may or may not contain apostrophe errors. Worksheets like this are readily available from any number of grammar/usage/mechanics teacher resources, including many free online sources.

Invent a New Way to Show Ownership

Students invent a new and different way to show ownership by completing the following exercise. Make copies of the following, and for enrichment give examples of other languages like Spanish, French, Italian, etc. that use a *de* to show possession - *casa de Pedro*.

> Let's face it: That thing we call the *apostrophe* is a random sign we use to show ownership. Other languages don't use apostrophes at all! Your job is to invent a new (and cool!) way to show ownership. For example, might you add a specific letter to the end word to show it belongs to that person? "I wrote to Joe and he wrote back. I received *Joe's letter*" then might become "I wrote to Joe and he wrote back. I received *letter-J*."
>
> Use your imagination! Dream up a new way of showing ownership.

A Few (Essential) Capitalization Rules

Rule #1: Capitalize the first word of a sentence.

- The car went zooming down the road.

Rule #2: DO capitalize all proper nouns, specific places, people, and things, *including name brands.*

- Chicago Sears Tower
- Oreo
- Dell
- Glenvar High School
- John Smith

Rule #3: Do NOT capitalize a word like *president, school,* or *war* unless it is referring to a *particular* one.

- The Civil War   *but*   We will soon go to war.
- President Lincoln   *but*   I'd like to be president.
- Williams Elementary School *but*   I like my elementary school.

Rule #4: DO capitalize all words that are a part of a person's title of address.

- I want to see Dr. Smith now. *but*   I want to see a doctor now.

Rule #5: DO capitalize any word that refers to a country, regional name, or language.

- I like Mexican food.
- I drove an Italian car.
- I like the people in the South.

Rule #6: Do NOT capitalize subjects in school unless they are referring to a language or have a number of some sort after them.

- I like English and Spanish, but I prefer to study chemistry, history, art, and Algebra II.

Capitalization Scavenger Hunt

Students go through magazines, newspapers, etc. and look for examples of capitalization rules being used in context. Have the students cut them out, and paste them to a sheet, categorizing them according to the rules they illustrate.

Scattergory ® !

For this activity, the teacher first needs to make a set of alphabet cards. Simply write the letters of the alphabet on 26 different index cards. (Remove the ones deemed too difficult for this activity.)

Given a set of alphabet cards and working in pairs or groups of three, students take turns drawing a card, and then individually, after the card is shown, each student brainstorms six (6) nouns they can think of that start with the drawn letter – with the following caveats:

❖ Each round's brainstorming time only lasts two minutes.
❖ In the first round, at least 2 of the nouns must use capitalization rule #1. Others may be uncapitalized.
❖ In the second round, at least 2 of the nouns must use capitalization rule #2.
❖ Game continues in likewise fashion until the teacher-specified number of rounds is completed.
❖ Students compare their lists after each round and then turn them into the teacher who may check for accuracy.

Example (*for Round Two*): if the letter **S** is drawn, a student might create the following list:

salt   **spinach**   **Sears**   **sand**   **scent**   **Sycamore Street**

Task
#3

Fill in the Blanks

Students complete **Fill-in-the-Blanks** exercises (modeled below), paying close attention to proper application and justification of the capitalization rules.

Example: S_____ a_____ s_____ s_____ o_____ T_____ .
Sally ate some spinach on Tuesday.

1. A_____ d_____ t_____ s_____ M_____ .

2. D_____ y_____ c_____ m_____ ?

3. S_____ f_____ t_____ C_____'s c_____ .

4. H_____ M_____ s_____ T_____!

5. G_____ m_____ J_____ a____ T_____ M_____ S_____ .

Once the students have completed the above Fill-in-the-Blank exercises, they may create some of their own to be completed by their classmates.

A Few (Essential) Comma Rules

Rule #1: Place a comma between the day and year in a date.

- I was born June 22, 1970.

Rule #2: Use a comma to offset nonessential introductory words or phrases that start a sentence.

- Without even looking, I could tell that my sister had entered the room.
- Yes, you may go to the dance.

Rule #3: Use commas to separate parts of an address, including cities and states.

- I used to live in Sunnyvale, Michigan, before I moved to Appleton, Montana.

Rule #4: Use commas to separate items in a series or a list.

- I like cherries, apples, and bananas. I also like to run 5 miles each day, take hot showers, and surf the internet.

Rule #5: Use commas to offset a person's name from the rest of the sentence when they are being directly addressed.

- Michael, I asked you to turn off the light.
- I asked you to go down to the store, Danielle.
- The other day I was thinking, Joshua, that maybe we should paint your room.

Rule #6: Use commas to separate extra, non-essential information found in a sentence.

- Uncle Jerry, whose hair is thinning, dislikes being compared to a bald eagle.

Standard Sentence Correction

Students will practice correcting given sentences that address and apply the essential comma rules. Worksheets like this are readily available from any number of grammar/usage/mechanics teacher resources, including many free online sources.

Roll the Dice

Pairs of students take turns rolling a pair of different-colored dice one of which is white. Leaving the dice where they land, the student who rolled them attempts to create a simple math problem (using multiplication or addition) whose answer is between 6 and 15. He or she rolls the dice until a 6 or 15 can be produced.

Then each person in the pair must individually create a complete sentence that includes the number of words specified on the dice. For example, if a 3 and 5 were rolled, a sentence of either 8 or 15 words might be created. The students' sentences must also include the use of the comma rule shown on the white die. For example, if the white die shows 5, then the students' sentences must show the correct use of Comma Rule #5 from the list above.

❖ I was thinking that you, Mark, should leave. (8 words)

❖ Mary, I was thinking about that time we went to that little restaurant in Chicago. (15 words)

Task
#3

Comma Craziness

Directions: Closely examine the following sentences. In each case, a comma could be placed strategically in such a way as to alter the meaning of the sentence. Play around with the possibilities, and, for each sentence, discover at least one way that a sentence's meaning could be altered by the addition of a comma. Then explain the differences in meaning between the original form and the new form. Describe that difference in words and then illustrate it.

Be creative with your approach, and use your imagination.

Example: You make me dinner!

Currently **means:** Someone is making the speaker of the sentence into dinner.

Picture idea: A drawing of a baked potato saying this line: "You make me dinner!"

You, make me dinner!

Now **means:** Someone is commanding another to make dinner for him.

Picture idea: A drawing of a young child sitting in a high chair yelling this line at an adult.

1. John Paul read your book!

2. You light my fire.

3. May I call you Chris?

4. Let's eat Grandma!

5. Sopranos sing with feeling.

6. Dogs can't leave them alone.

7. He had his dinner on Josh.

8. She had three toed sloths.

Nouns

Overview: *These readiness-based tasks give students a chance to identify nouns while working at appropriate levels of challenge.* The students work on these tasks following whole-group activities designed to introduce the nature and role of nouns, such as:

❖ Using a concept attainment activity to introduce nouns. In this type of activity, a teacher shares a list of words that are nouns (the "IN" list) along with a list of words that are not nouns (the "OUT" list). Students are invited to add words to either list and to discover what it takes to be included on the "IN" list,

❖ Reading Brian Cleary's A Mink, a Fink, a Skating Rink or parts of Ruth Heller's Merry-Go-Round,

❖ Creating a class "noun web,"

❖ Brainstorming, either as a whole group or in small groups, nouns that fit into broad categories (for example, people, places, animals, things) or more specific categories (jobs that people might have, cities and towns, ocean animals, tools).

Assign students to the tiered tasks below based on teacher observation of their grasp of nouns during introductory activities and on their general reading and writing ability.

Standard:

➢ Apply grammar and language conventions to communicate effectively

Objectives:

The students will **KNOW**

• People, places, and things are *nouns*.

The students will **UNDERSTAND THAT**

• Sentences are made up of different types of words, and each word in a sentence has a job.

The students will **BE ABLE TO**

• Identify nouns.

• Categorize words.

Materials:

• Sentences written on chart paper (include different types of nouns in the sentences: people, places, and things)

• Word splash including nouns and other parts of speech (A word splash is a collection of words that are randomly placed on a page and that may or may not have something in common.)

• Short sentences written on sentence strips and cut into pieces representing subjects, verbs, and prepositional phrases

---

Tier One (lower readiness)

Students assigned to this tier work as a group with the teacher (or another adult) to identify nouns in sentences written on chart paper. Students underline or circle the nouns that they find. Once they have found all the nouns, they look for relationships among them. *Do some of the nouns seem to go together? How?* When they have finished, the students may illustrate some of the nouns that they found. If they are able to do so, have them label their illustrations.

Tier Two (middle readiness)

Students working on this task work with a partner or independently to pick nouns out of a group of different words provided on a word splash. Once they have circled all of the nouns on the word splash, they group the nouns into at least three different categories. They list their groups on a separate sheet of paper, making sure to provide a label or title for each group. Once finished, they share their groupings with others working at this same tier.

Tier Three (higher readiness)

Students at this tier work in pairs and use parts of sentences written on sentence strips to create their own complete sentences. As they create their sentences, have them write them. Once they have created and written at least six sentences, they circle the nouns in them. They then create categories for their nouns. *Which ones seem to go together? Why?* Ask them to list at least three categories and name the categories.

Closure: Once students have completed their assigned tasks, the teacher leads a whole-group discussion to review nouns and discuss their importance:
- What are some of the nouns that you found when you were working on your activity?
- Why are nouns important? What would it be like without nouns?
- What are some of your favorite nouns? Why?

Reference Materials

Overview: *These tiered activities give students an opportunity to explore or apply their understandings of the dictionary as a reference resource.* At each tier, students work on identifying the essential features of a dictionary. Assign students to the appropriate assignments based on the students' grasp of the dictionary's unique features and their comfort level with skills such as alphabetizing.

Standards:
  ➢ Use word-reference materials, including the dictionary
  ➢ Use text organizers, such as type, headings, and graphics, to categorize information
  ➢ Use knowledge of word origins; synonyms, antonyms, and homonyms; and multiple meanings of words

Objectives:

The students will **KNOW**
  • Parts of speech, including nouns, verbs, adjectives, adverbs.
  • The uses of a dictionary.

The students will **UNDERSTAND THAT**
  • The dictionary is a highly organized non-fiction reference resource that is designed to help the user understand the meanings and pronunciation of unfamiliar words.
  • Text set in special type styles (e.g., boldfaced, italics) and even pictures help to convey information.
  • Diacritical marks help the user of a dictionary discover acceptable pronunciation of unfamiliar words.

The students will **BE ABLE TO**
  • Use both context and the dictionary to clarify the meaning of unfamiliar words.
  • Identify and use a dictionary's features, such as guide words, to find a word and understand its meaning.

Materials:
- A set of classroom dictionaries
- Copies of the following three worksheets:

Tier One (lower readiness): *"Dictionary Scavenger Hunt"*

Tier Two (middle readiness): *"Using the Dictionary"*

Tier Three (higher readiness): *"You Are Webster"*

Closure: In addition to checking the worksheets for accuracy, pose the following questions to the whole class:
- When should you use a dictionary?
- What kind of information does a dictionary provide?
- Where else might you find this kind of information?

Dictionary Scavenger Hunt

1. Look on page _____ of the dictionary. Write down the two **guide words** that appear at the top of the page.

_____ and _____

2. Use the page diagram on the right and now show where else those two guide words are found. Indicate with an 'X' for each guide word.

3. Write the **definition** of the first word on the page in the space below.

4. Write two other words that appear on the page, in the order that they appear on the page.

_____ and _____

5. Look up the definition of the word *run*. It appears on page _____.

❖ What are the two guide words for that page? _____

_____

❖ How many definitions are there for the word *run*? _____

6. Choose one of those many definitions, and write a sentence that shows a meaning of the word *run* that is *different from* "moving swiftly on foot." Write that sentence in the space below.

7. Look up the word *anthem*. Write the pronunciation guide that appears right after the word in parentheses. In the space below, write it exactly as it appears in the dictionary, including all those unusual **diacritical marks**.

❖ Using what you know about the way the word *anthem* is pronounced, which of the following words have a sound like the one indicated by the symbol **ə**? Circle them.

hymn   glum   python   use   take   lift   fork

❖ In the space below, write any other word you can think of that has the **ə** sound.

_____

❖ How many **syllables** are in the word *anthem*? _____

8. Flip through the dictionary until you find a word that is illustrated with a **picture**. In the space below, draw a simple sketch of what you see there, and label it with the word.

10. Now, flip through the dictionary again and look for a word whose meaning you do not already know. In the box:

❖ Write the two guide words where they belong.
❖ Write the word.
❖ Write the pronunciation of that word and its definition.
❖ Draw a picture that helps to illustrate the word.

Using the Dictionary

The following comment was written by Johnny's teacher on his last report card. Read it carefully, using the dictionary to look up any words with meanings that confuse you. Then answer the questions on the next page on a separate piece of paper (unless otherwise noted).

Dear Mr. and Mrs. Smith:

Johnny has been very loquacious for the past 9 weeks, especially when he is working at his table with others. He is easily diverted from the tasks we do in class, and as a result, I must goad him to stay on task. The vociferous nature of his voice can be quite distracting to the other students who need a more serene environment in which to work.

I am bewildered by how to best encourage him to be attentive while at school. He often becomes engrossed with doodling in his notebook, rather than completing the assignment presented to him. I attribute his interest in drawing to his mother, who I know is an art teacher at another elementary school. While I admire his artistic prowess, I cannot allow him to make illustrations in his textbooks, which I have ascertained he is doing – two of his table partners confirmed this for me.

Johnny works a bit too quickly. He needs to slow down and heed the directions provided for each assignment. Two days ago, he turned in an essay that had clearly been hastily written. It was full of mistakes and was unorganized. The handwriting was atrocious, too.

Johnny is a fine person. He is never sullen, and he always has a comical remark to make. The other students in the class find him to be quite charismatic. I enjoy his personality a great deal, but I do have some worry that Johnny might have some deficiencies in his school work next year as a sixth grader if his study habits do not improve.

Please speak with him about these problems at home, and let me know your thoughts.

Sincerely,

--Ms. Stickler

1. In the first paragraph, Ms. Stickler says that *"Johnny has been very loquacious for the past 9 weeks."* Draw a picture that illustrates what this means.

2. Based on your reading, what are some things Johnny does that *divert* him from the tasks at hand?

3. If you were Ms. Stickler, what sorts of actions might you take to *goad* Johnny to stay on task? List and describe three actions.

   1.

   2.

   3.

4. Based on the reading, which of the following words best describes Johnny's voice? Circle the answer.

high-pitched squeaky   unusually loud   quiet, soft   scratchy, gruff

5. List a place in your school that is usually *serene*.

6. Ms. Stickler writes in the second paragraph that she is **"bewildered** *by how to best encourage him to be attentive while at school."* What does this mean?

7. What are some things **you** enjoy doing that really *engross* you the way Johnny's drawing does for him?

8. Ms. Stickler writes, *"I admire his artistic prowess."* Which of the following is the best word to express the meaning of *prowess*? Circle the best answer.

materials   ideas   ability   personality   painting

9. Ms. Stickler says that two of Johnny's table mates helped her *ascertain* he was doodling in the textbooks. How would you feel if you were Johnny and those two people had helped Ms. Stickler ascertain this information?

10. Ms. Stickler seems to think that Johnny would do better if he would only *heed the directions*. What does this mean?

What might happen if you do not heed a stop sign?

11. Give an example of what Johnny's handwriting might look like based on what you read in the third paragraph.

12. Ms. Stickler says that Johnny is never *sullen*. That's a good thing! On the back of this paper draw a picture of what a sullen person's face might look like.

13. Ms. Stickler writes, *"The other students in the class find him to be quite **charismatic**."* Which of the following is the best word to express the meaning of *charismatic*? Circle the best answer.

annoying   funny   likeable   disgusting   crazy

You Are Webster!

There are over 600,000 words in the English language. That is a huge number, and yet every year new words are coined and added to our language. Recent additions include words like *bling,* meaning "any type of gaudy, showy jewelry" and *google,* a word that describes the act of searching for information online. The fact is, words spring up around us every day. Whether or not they are adopted by our culture depends on how popular they become.

Your job is to **invent and define 10 new words** that could be used around school and then write a dictionary-style entry for each. Each entry must include the following:

- ❖ Two guide words that would help a person locate your special word in a dictionary
- ❖ The word, as it would be spelled by you
- ❖ The pronunciation of the word, using any diacritical marks (use a real dictionary to help you with this!)
- ❖ The part of speech of the word (is it a noun? a verb? an adjective or adverb?)
- ❖ The meaning of the word
- ❖ An example of a sentence that uses the new word in context and thereby illustrates its meaning
- ❖ ALL of the 10 words must be listed in alphabetical order when you are finished.

To get your creative juices flowing, think about all the unusual things that might happen at school. Do we need a word for the sound of the teacher's voice as she calls the class in from recess? What about a word to describe the look on her face when a student has done something wrong? What about the cafeteria? Are there any words we might need to describe certain smells there? Be creative!

The example below will show what your entry should look like.

flag	**flaunt**
flam·er·cite·ment (flăm-ûr-sīt'měnt) *n.* the excess energy children in school have after returning to the classroom from a fire drill.	
The flamercitement in the room made it difficult for the teacher to get her class to concentrate on the math lesson.	

Synonyms

Overview: *These tiered activities provide practice with identifying and using synonyms. Prior to working on their assigned tasks, introduce students to the term synonym (a word that means the same thing as another word) and provide basic instruction in identifying pairs/groups of synonyms.* This may include providing pairs of common synonyms and asking the students how they are related.

Standards:
- ➢ Develop an extensive vocabulary
- ➢ Engage in word play

Objectives:

The students will **KNOW**
- *Synonyms* are words that mean the same thing.

The students will **UNDERSTAND THAT**
- Different words can mean basically the same thing.
- Writers and speakers choose words to make their writing and speaking more interesting to their readers and listeners.

The students will **BE ABLE TO**
- Identify and select synonyms.
- Use synonyms in phrases.

Materials:
- Several sets of index cards, each card showing a word that is one-half of a pair of synonyms (for example, *large* and *big*, *pretty* and *beautiful*) for "Synonym Concentration"
- Sentence strips showing phrases (allow for multiple synonyms to be inserted into the phrases, such as "a *pretty* day" or "a *loud* dog")

Closure: Have students suggest adjectives – describing words. Write them on the board. While writing the words on the board, ask students to select one of the words from the group of words. For example, the adjective *huge*. Have students suggest synonyms for *huge*. Then ask students to identify the best synonym from their suggestions. Once the students have identified the best synonym and have explained why they chose it, ask them to brainstorm more synonyms for *huge*. This process can be repeated as often as needed.

© Pieces of Learning

Tier One (lower readiness)

Students assigned to this tier, most likely non-readers and/or second language learners, work with a teacher. Given a phrase such as "a large building," they illustrate the phrase and then discuss other ways to describe their illustrations. For example, they may come up with "a big building" or "a gigantic building." Go through this process several times using a variety of phrases such as:

✓ A pretty dress
✓ The mean dog
✓ A fast car
✓ A scary monster

Tier Two (middle readiness)

Students working at this tier play "Synonym Concentration" in small groups of two or three students. Given a set of several pairs of synonyms (at least ten), they take turns trying to match the pairs of synonyms by recalling where they are and turning the cards over to check if they are right. The winner is the student who successfully matches the most pairs. Give the students extra blank index cards, and encourage them to add more pairs of synonyms to the game before playing it again.

Tier Three (higher readiness)

Students assigned to this tier brainstorm as many ways as they can to say the same phrase. For example, given a phrase such as "a pretty day," they create a list of possible ways to say it without changing its meaning. Provide students with several phrases written on sentence strips. If they are able, the students may use dictionaries to generate more ideas. Additional possible phrases include:

✓ A loud dog
✓ A bad day
✓ The rough ocean
✓ The dirty dishes

Notes

Readiness-Based Math Tiered Assignments

Addition and Subtraction of Whole Numbers

Overview: *These tiered activities give students independent practice with adding and subtracting whole numbers while working at appropriate levels of challenge.* Do not assign these tasks until students have become familiar with the addition and subtraction algorithms and have had some practice using them. If addition skills are the focus, eliminate the subtraction portion of the tiers.

Standards:
> ➤ Solve problems involving the sum or difference of whole numbers using paper and pencil methods
> ➤ Develop fluency with multi-digit addition and subtraction problems

Objectives:

The students will **KNOW**
- Before adding and subtracting with paper and pencil, addition and subtraction problems expressed in horizontal form should be rewritten in vertical form by lining up the places vertically.
- Flexible methods of adding and subtracting whole numbers can be developed by taking apart and combining numbers in a variety of ways, most depending on place value.

The students will **UNDERSTAND THAT**
- Addition involves combining quantities, and subtraction involves separating quantities.
- Addition and subtraction are inverse operations.

The students will **BE ABLE TO**
- Determine the sum or difference of whole numbers in vertical form with or without regrouping.
- Determine the sum or difference of whole numbers in horizontal form with or without regrouping.
- Find the sum or difference of whole numbers using paper and pencil.

Materials:
- Paper and pencil
- Decks of playing cards for Tier One

Tier One (lower readiness)

Students working at this tier will be assigned at the teacher's discretion to either a pair or small group no larger than four. This tier involves both collaborative and independent work. Each partner team or small group is given a deck of playing cards. The numbered cards are assigned the value of the card. Face cards have the following values:

Jack = 11

Queen = 12

King = 13

Ace = either 1 or 14, depending upon the readiness of the group

One student in each pair or small group shuffles the deck of cards and deals out five cards per student. The remaining cards are placed in a pile face down. Each student writes the value of the five cards in his or her hand, adds these five values using pencil and paper, and records the sum. The players take turns drawing a new card from the pile in front of them. Each player has the option of adding or subtracting the card's value from the sum already recorded from the opening hand of five cards.

The goal is to reach a given value as closely as possible. The teacher sets this value, depending upon the number of students in each group and their readiness in working with larger numbers. The teacher also has the option of determining the length of this activity. Students play until all the cards have been drawn from the pile, or they can draw five more cards after the initial hand is dealt. This is determined by how many students are playing together. The winning student is the one who by adding or subtracting comes closest to the pre-determined value. After a student has won, cards can be reshuffled and students may play another round if time permits.

At the end of class, students give the teacher the papers showing their calculations. These can be used for assessment.

Tier Two (higher readiness)

Students assigned to this tier work independently.

Starting with A = 1, students write the alphabet and assign a numerical value to each letter in sequential order. Have each student complete this task with Z = 26.

After they have listed a one-to-one correspondence with letters and numbers, students select ten of their classmates who can be working at either tier. They then add the value of those students' first and last names using pencil and paper. For example, if a student were named Ann Smith, the numerical value of her name would be:

A   N   N   S   M   I   T   H
1 + 14 +14 + 19 + 13 + 9 + 20 + 8 = 98

(Note: Students would be expected to line up these values vertically before adding.)

Once students have calculated the numerical value of ten names, they are given a predetermined numerical goal such as 175. The teacher may set this goal at any value. Students, through trial and error methods, must determine which two of the ten student name values can be added or subtracted to come closest to the given numerical goal. The winning student is the one who by adding or subtracting comes closest to the pre-determined value set by the teacher.

At the end of class, students give the teacher the papers showing their calculations. These can be used for assessment.

Closure: Students come back together as a whole group. The teacher selects several students from each tier to describe their activity to the other tier. The winners from each activity are announced. They share with the rest of the class how close they came to the teacher-determined numerical goals and the strategies they used that helped them get there.

Comparing Standard and Metric Measurement

Overview: *These tiered activities provide students with the opportunity to apply their knowledge of the U.S. customary and metric systems of measurement in situations where actual measurement and estimation are required.* Offer these assignments after instruction of measurement skills is completed. Assign students to tiers based upon their accurate and effective use of measuring tools and their estimation skills. They may work independently or with a partner to complete the tasks, as determined by the teacher.

Standards:
➢ Estimate and measure length, using actual measuring tools, and describe the results in both metric and U.S. Customary units, including parts of an inch, inches, feet, yards, millimeters, centimeters, and meters
➢ Estimate the conversion of inches and centimeters, yards and meters, using approximate comparisons

Objectives:
The students will **KNOW**
- *Length* is the distance along a line or figure from one point to another.
- U.S. customary units for measurement of length include inches, feet, yards, and miles. Appropriate measuring tools include rulers, yardsticks, and tape measures.
- Metric units for measurement of length include millimeters, centimeters, meters, and kilometers. Appropriate measuring tools include centimeter rulers, meter sticks, and metric tape measures.

The students will **UNDERSTAND THAT**
- The context and intent of the measuring problem determines which measuring tool and unit of measure will be used to solve it.
- Practical experience measuring familiar objects helps establish benchmarks and facilitates the ability to use units of measure to make estimates.
- Relationships exist between U.S. customary units of measure and metric units of measure.

The students will **BE ABLE TO**
- Use appropriate measurement tools to measure the length of everyday objects in U.S. customary units, expressing the length in parts of an inch, inches, feet, and yards.
- Use appropriate measurement tools to measure the length of everyday objects in metric units, expressing the length in millimeters, centimeters, and meters.
- Make ballpark comparisons to estimate conversion between standard and metric measurement units.

© Pieces of Learning

Materials:
- Standard rulers
- Metric rulers
- Yardsticks
- Meter sticks
- Standard and metric tape measures, if available
- Paper and pencil
- A variety of objects to measure

(Note: You may want to bring a collection of items from home if your classroom does not provide enough variety for these measurement activities.)

Tier One (lower readiness)

The students working at this tier are having difficulty using measurement tools to make accurate measurements. Their tasks focus on the accurate use of measurement tools.

Choose ten very different items in the classroom. These items might come from your backpack, the shelves and counters in the room, the furniture, or they might be selected from items that your teacher has brought into the classroom specifically for this lesson. Choose different-sized items that have straight edges. Your job is to use the tools provided by your teacher to accurately measure twice the length and width of each of your ten objects.

You will first measure each object using U.S. customary units. You must decide whether inches, feet, or yards is the best unit for recording your answer. You will make the second measurement of each object using metric units. Again, you must select the best metric unit for measuring each object: millimeters, centimeters, or meters. Construct a chart that shows the name of the object you measured, its length and width in U.S. customary units, and its length and width in metric units. Record your measurements on the chart, and give it to your teacher when it is completed.

Tier Two (middle readiness)

Choose ten very different items in the classroom. These items might come from your backpack, the shelves and counters in the room, the furniture, or they might be selected from items that your teacher has brought into the classroom specifically for this lesson. Choose different-sized items that have straight edges. Your job is to estimate twice the length and width of each object. One of your estimations will be made using a metric unit of measure and one will use a U.S. customary unit of measure. You must decide which unit is appropriate for each object. Before making your estimations, use measuring tools to observe the size of an inch, foot, yard, millimeter, centimeter, and meter. You will use these observations as a basis for estimating.

Once your estimations are complete, use measurement tools to measure the actual length and width of each object. Construct a chart to record the objects you chose to measure, your estimates, and the objects' actual measurements. Calculate the difference between the two measurements, and indicate whether each estimate was too long or too short. Record this information on your chart. Give your chart to your teacher when it is completed.

Tier Three (higher readiness)

The goal of the tasks at this tier is for students to make ballpark comparisons between measurement systems and not to memorize conversion factors between U.S. customary and metric units.

Choose ten very different items in the classroom. These items might come from your backpack, the shelves and counters in the room, the furniture, or they might be selected from items that your teacher has brought into the classroom specifically for this lesson. Choose different-sized items that have straight edges. Your first task is to accurately measure the length and width of each object using U.S. customary units. Your second task is to use ballpark comparisons to convert your U.S. customary measurements to metric measurements. One inch is about 2 1/2 (2.5) centimeters, and about 1 1/10 yards equals a meter. In other words, a meter is just slightly longer than a yard. Use these comparisons to estimate the metric measurements of your objects. If your measurements are in feet, convert them to inches before estimating the metric measure.

Your next task is to use a metric measurement tool and measure the actual length and width of your objects in metric units. Construct a chart to record the objects you chose to measure, their U.S. customary measurements, your estimated metric conversions, and the actual metric measurements. Calculate the difference between the estimated metric measurement and the actual metric measurement. Indicate whether each estimated conversion was too long or too short. Record this information on your chart. Give your chart to your teacher when it is completed.

Closure: Display the students' charts around the classroom for students in each tier to compare/contrast their chosen objects, estimates, and measurements. Discuss with the students within each tier what difficulties they faced completing their tasks. The whole class can address the following issue: Since the United States is one of the few countries in the world that doesn't use metric measure for all measurement tasks, should we only use metric measure and eliminate U.S. customary measure? Why or why not?

Coordinate Graphing

Overview: *These readiness-based assignments give students an opportunity to apply their knowledge of the two-dimensional coordinate graphing system.* Students complete their chosen tasks either individually or with a partner working at their same readiness level. Introduce these tiered activities after students have been introduced to coordinate graphing and have had practice reading and locating points on a grid.

Standards:
- ➤ Identify the ordered pair for a point, and locate the point for an ordered pair on a two-dimensional grid
- ➤ Use two-dimensional coordinate grids to represent points and graph lines and simple figures

Objectives:

The students will **KNOW**
- A *coordinate grid* is a way to locate points in a plane.
- The horizontal number line is called the *x-axis* or the *horizontal axis,* and the vertical number line is called the *y-axis* or the *vertical axis*.
- Any point on a coordinate plane can be named with two numbers called an *ordered pair* or *coordinates*.

The students will **UNDERSTAND THAT**
- A pair of numbers on a coordinate plane corresponds to one and only one point on the grid.
- In an ordered pair (x,y), x represents the location along the horizontal axis and y represents the location along the vertical axis.
- When plotting a point on the grid, one must always start at the origin $(0,0)$.

The students will **BE ABLE TO**
- Identify the ordered pair for a point on a coordinate plane, given the coordinates (x,y).
- Locate points on a coordinate grid, given the coordinates (x,y).
- Describe the path between given points on the coordinate plane.

Materials:
- Copies of coordinate grid paper
- Rulers for a straight edge
- Pencils or colored pencils

Tier One (lower readiness)

Students at this tier practice naming and locating coordinate points on a grid by playing the game *Battleship*. If the teacher is unfamiliar with the rules of this game, an Internet search for "Battleship rules" will locate multiple sites that offer easy explanations. Students are paired with a partner to play the game.

Each student is given a sheet of coordinate grid paper. The x-axis and y-axis can either be preprinted on the grid or the students can draw them using a straight edge. Students will utilize the number of grid quadrants that have been introduced in class. For lower-readiness learners, the first quadrant (all positive values) will probably be the only one drawn. Students create a fleet of ships using a submarine, a destroyer, and a carrier. These ships are located on the grid by choosing two adjacent coordinate points for a submarine, three adjacent coordinate points for a destroyer, and four points for a carrier. As the opponent calls out the coordinates of a grid point, the player responds by calling out a hit or a miss. At the end of a predetermined time, the player who has sunk the most ships wins. The game can be repeated several times to offer the necessary practice in locating and naming points.

Tier Two (middle readiness)

Each student at this tier is given a piece of coordinate grid paper and a straight edge. The x-axis and y-axis can either be preprinted on the grid or the students can draw them. Students will utilize the number of grid quadrants that have been introduced in class.

Each student uses the straight edge to draw a figure on the grid whose sides pass through multiple coordinate points. The shape of the figure is at the discretion of the student. A point is drawn at each vertex of the figure and other points can be identified along the sides until the student has located 15 points around the perimeter of the figure. On a separate piece of paper, the student names each coordinate pair that represents a point on the figure. After the first point is named, the student names the other fourteen points in order as they occur around the perimeter, ending with the same point that was identified first. This list of coordinates is then given to a partner along with another piece of grid paper with the axes either identified or drawn. The partner plots the coordinates and connects each point in the order listed. The goal is for the partner's figure to be identical to the original figure.

Tier Three (higher readiness)

Each student at this tier is given a piece of coordinate grid paper and a straight edge. The x-axis and y-axis can either be preprinted on the grid or the students can draw them. Students will utilize the number of grid quadrants that have been introduced in class.

Ask the students to assume the role of a spy. The role can be associated with the Revolutionary War, the Civil War, a modern spy, or a character from a novel that the students have read. On a separate sheet of paper, compose a short message appropriate to the spy's role. This message will be coded using coordinate points. Students count the number of different letters used in the message. If there are 18 different letters used, the student draws 18 different points spread around the grid and labels each one with one of the letters in the message. On a separate sheet of paper, the student writes out the message in code, using a letter's coordinates instead of the letter. For example, if the first word in the message is "Send," the code would be written as:

_____ _____ _____ _____ , with "S" being located at (4,2) on the grid, "E" located at (3,1) etc.
(4,2)   (3,1)   (6,7)   (0,8)

Each student then exchanges the grid and coded message with a partner who will decode the message by matching the coordinates with the letters on the grid.

Closure: Closure will occur within each of the readiness tiers instead of bringing the class together as a whole. At each level, students can share what strategies worked best for completing their assigned tasks and what strategies were unsuccessful. They can also share any problems that occurred in naming and locating coordinate points.

Counting by 2s, 5s, and 10s

Overview: *These tasks allow students to practice different counting patterns while working at appropriate levels of challenge based on their readiness levels.* Prior to working on these tasks, give students experiences with counting on number lines and on number grids and practice using counting patterns in whole and small group activities.

Standards:
  ➢ Read, write, and model numbers through 100
  ➢ Recognize patterns in numbers

Objectives:
The students will **KNOW**
  • Numbers 1 through 100.
The students will **UNDERSTAND THAT**
  • Counting patterns help us make predictions about numbers.
  • There are different types of counting patterns.
The students will **BE ABLE TO**
  • Count by 2s, 5s, and 10s.
  • Make predictions.
  • Create patterns.

Materials:
  • Dot-to-dots using counting by 2s, 5s, and 10s (available in teacher supply stores and bookstores)
  • Blank paper
  • Tracing paper
  • Number grids
  • Colored pencils

Closure: When the students have completed their assigned tasks, they will form a large circle to play a "standup/sit down" game. As you count from 1, they will either stand up or sit down when you come to a number that falls in the 5s pattern. For example, if they begin sitting down, they will stand on 5, will sit on 10, will stand on 15, etc.

Tier One (lower readiness)

Students assigned to this tier work independently to complete dot-to-dots that highlight counting by 2s, 5s, and 10s. When they have successfully completed at least two of each, they create their own dot-to-dots using the following process (model this process for the students):

1) Draw a simple picture on a blank sheet of paper.
2) Place a piece of tracing paper over the picture.
3) Place dots on the tracing paper showing different points on the picture.
4) Pick a starting point and an ending point.
5) Label the dots with numbers (2s, 5s, and 10s), making sure to put them in the correct order so that the picture can be drawn correctly.

Make copies of the students' dot-to-dots so they can share them with their classmates and families.

Tier Two (middle readiness)

Students assigned to this tier show counting patterns using number grids (1 to 100) and colored pencils. Represent each counting pattern with a different color. Each student will have his or her own grid, and the students may work in pairs to color spaces that they come to when they count by 2s. Then they will do the same for 5s and 10s. Encourage the students to challenge one another to guess which numbers will come next. Do the students begin to see a pattern in the colored spaces? How can they use this pattern to make predictions? As they identify a pattern, can they determine whether or not a large number will be part of the pattern? For example, will they come to 76 when counting by 2s? How about by 5s and 10s? How do they know?

Tier Three (higher readiness)

Given a number grid (1 to 100), students assigned to this tier work in small groups of two to three students to figure out which numbers would be found in all of the patterns (2s, 5s, and 10s). Once they have decided on these numbers, they begin to color the grid using only one color to highlight the numbers found in all three patterns. Were their predictions correct? Did they identify the correct numbers?

Next, the students will work independently to complete number patterns that include blanks. Provide a range of patterns, requiring counting by 2s, 5s, and 10s from any number and increasing in difficulty. Examples include:

16, _____, 20, _____, 24, _____

35, _____, _____, 50, _____, 60

40, _____, _____, _____, _____, 90

44, 46, _____, _____, _____, 54, _____, _____

When the students have successfully completed a range of patterns, they may create their own patterns for other students to complete who are working at this tier.

Decimal Number Sense

Overview: *These tiered activities provide students with the opportunity to apply their knowledge of decimal place value, reading decimals, and writing decimals.* The readiness level for the activities is determined by the fluency with which students can read and write decimal values. Prior to assigning these tasks, introduce students to decimal place value and practice reading and writing decimal amounts up to the thousandths place. Students in *Tier One* work in partner teams, and students in *Tier Two* work independently.

Standards:
- ➤ Read, write, and identify the place values of decimal amounts through thousandths
- ➤ Build understanding of the relationship between whole number and decimal place value

Objectives:

The students will **KNOW**
- A decimal point separates the whole number places from the places less than one.
- A number containing a decimal point is called a decimal number or simply a *decimal*.
- Decimals may be written in place value format (4.3) or using words (four and three tenths.)

The students will **UNDERSTAND THAT**
- The structure of the base-10 whole number system is based upon a simple pattern of tens in which each place is ten times the value of the place to its right.
- The structure of the base-10 decimal number system is based upon the inverse of the whole number place names.
- Place values extend infinitely in two directions from a decimal point.

The students will **BE ABLE TO**
- Identify the place values for each digit in decimals through thousandths.
- Read decimal numbers through thousandths shown in written words or in place-value format.
- Write decimal numbers through thousandths in written words or given decimal numbers presented orally.

Materials:
- Egg cartons (Remove the lid and cut the base in half lengthwise so that each player has one row with six sections)
- Small pieces of construction paper or tag board
- Dice or number cubes labeled 1-6
- Any kind of chips, counters, or dried beans
- Copies of sport magazines or newspapers
- Internet access

Tier One (lower readiness)

Students assigned to this tier play a game in pairs to practice reading and writing whole number values and decimal values through thousandths. If the tier has an odd number of members, two students of equal readiness can play on the same team. Each player receives half of a plastic egg carton that has been cut so that each player has a row with six sections. Each student will make the following labels to place in front of the six sections of the egg carton in the given order:

Hundreds	Tens	Ones	Tenths	Hundredths	Thousandths

Students are given a pile of chips, beans, etc. Players roll the die, and the player with the highest number goes first. Students receive these directions: The goal is to build a greater number in the egg carton than your opponent. For example, suppose the first player rolls the die and a 5 is showing. That player takes 5 chips and puts them in one of the place value sections of the egg carton. Remember that the goal is to create a number that is larger than the opponent's. Now, suppose the second player rolls a 3 and places 3 chips in one of his or her egg carton sections. Play continues until all the sections of both opponents' egg cartons are filled. Each player writes the decimal value formed and then reads the value to the other player. The student with the largest value wins. The teacher can determine the number of rounds each pair plays or can set a time limit and allow pairs to play as many rounds as possible during the allotted time. After play stops, students turn in to the teacher the written decimal values that they formed during the game.

Tier Two (higher readiness)

Students assigned to this tier will be utilizing real world uses of decimal values and researching data using the Internet to complete the following assignment:

Your task is to assume the role of a coach. You may pick the sport that you are coaching, so choose one in which you have an interest. It can be a boys' or a girls' team. The sport must use decimal values in its record keeping, but almost every sport does. You will be giving a short speech to the members of your team, summarizing your season and mentioning all of the records set by team members this year. In your speech, you must use at least ten different decimal values with a mix of place names as you talk about records and statistics. Once you have decided on the sport that you will be coaching, visit some web sites that offer sports records and statistics to get a feel for the kinds of numbers associated with your sport. For example, if you choose to coach soccer, type "soccer records" or "soccer statistics" into your search engine to find sites to visit. You may also talk about famous players in your speech and mention records that they set. Each sport has its own magazine. If you can find one for your sport, it will give you ideas for your decimal uses. When your speech is written, share it with other members of your class.

Closure: For *Tier One*, the teacher can lead a debriefing discussion that addresses any difficulties students had forming and reading their decimal values. Students may also share any strategies they used in trying to form a larger number than their opponents'. For *Tier Two*, students read their speeches aloud either to the other members of their tier or to the whole class.

Graphing and Data Analysis

Overview: *These tiered activities provide students with the opportunity to apply their knowledge of graphing and data collection and are differentiated based on the complexity of the types of data collected at each tier.* The teacher assigns these tasks after instruction about reading and constructing bar graphs is completed. Students work independently or in cooperative learning groups to complete the tasks, as determined by the teacher.

Standards:
  ➤ Organize and display data in appropriate bar graphs
  ➤ Collect and organize data on a given topic using experiments, research, and surveys
  ➤ Read and interpret data represented in bar graphs, and use the display to interpret the results, draw conclusions, and make predictions

Objectives:

The students will **KNOW**
  • Data analysis helps describe data, recognize patterns or trends, and make predictions.
  • Bar graphs use parallel, horizontal, or vertical bars to represent counts for several categories. One bar is used for each category, with the length of the bar representing the count for that category.
  • Each axis of a bar graph should be labeled, and the graph should have a title.

The students will **UNDERSTAND THAT**
  • Bar graphs can be used to compare counts of different categories (categorical data).
  • Data displayed in bar graphs can be interpreted so that informed decisions can be made.
  • Conclusions and predictions can be justified by basing them on displays of data.

The students will **BE ABLE TO**
  • Collect data using observations, experiments, surveys, or research.
  • Construct and display data in bar graphs, labeling one axis with numerical data and the other axis with categories related to the content of the graph.
  • Create an appropriate title for a graph.
  • Compose a written description of one or more sentences to interpret the graph's data, as in, "The summer sport preferred by most is swimming."

Materials:
  • Collections of stackable items explained in the teacher note for *Tier One*
  • Grid paper appropriate for constructing bar graphs; paper for creating charts
  • Pencils, rulers, markers, or crayons
  • Internet access

(Note: At each of the three tiers, the teacher may determine whether students create their bar graphs using computer software or by hand using grid paper, rulers, and markers/crayons.)

Tier One (lower readiness)

(Note: Students working at this tier need a collection of ten different types of objects to stack, one on top of the other. The teacher can describe and model this activity a day before it occurs so that students can bring in some items from home. Suggestions for stackable items include color tiles, color cubes, Cuisenaire® rods, similar pattern block shapes, Life Savers© or other round candies, small cookies or crackers, poker chips, any flat math manipulative available in the classroom, paperback books, rulers, marshmallows, etc.)

Your task is to use the ten different groups of objects that you and your teacher have collected to create stacks. Suppose color cubes make up one of your collections of objects. You will carefully stack the cubes, one on top of each other, counting each new cube that is added to the stack. You may not mix the items in the stacks. Continue stacking and counting until the stack topples over. Create a chart to record your data. Write on your chart what you were stacking and how many objects were in the tower before it fell. Do not count the cube that caused the stack to fall. You will stack the other nine groups of objects in your collection in the same manner, recording the data on your chart. When you have finished stacking all ten groups of items, use the data in your chart to create a bar graph. Generate this graph using a computer program or design it on graph paper. Give the graph a title and label both the horizontal axis and vertical axis.

Compose a short paragraph explaining the results of your data by indicating which item built the tallest tower before falling over. Which was the easiest to stack? The hardest? Why?

Tier Two (middle readiness)

Choose one of the following sources to gather a set of data:

✓ The web site of a favorite sports team. The data may be generated by the team, such as win-loss records over a period of years, or by individual players.

✓ The Weather Channel web site. There is a wealth of weather data for individual cities listed here. The highs or lows of different cities can be compared, or you can collect data for one specific city. www.weather.com

✓ The United States Census Bureau's web site (www.census.gov) includes a large variety of data about people who live in the United States. Explore this web site to find a topic of interest to you.

✓ The Bureau of Transportation web site about airline statistics (www.bts.gov/programs/airline_information/)

✓ The World Almanac for Kids (www.worldalmanacforkids.com/explore/index.html)

After you have chosen a set of data, use it to create a bar graph. Generate this graph using a computer program or design it on graph paper. Give the graph a title and label both the horizontal axis and vertical axis. Once the graph is constructed, compose five interesting questions that can be answered using your graph's data. Trade your graph and questions with another student so that you each can interpret the other's graph.

Tier Three (higher readiness)

Choose a topic from the list below and conduct a survey of students in your school. Collect data from at least 15 students. Topics you may choose to survey include:

✓ What types of pets do you have in your home?

✓ Which ice cream flavor would be your first choice when ordering at an ice cream store? (Give students a choice from 10 popular flavors: vanilla, chocolate, butter pecan, strawberry, chocolate chip, cookies and cream, vanilla fudge ripple, pralines and cream, mint chocolate chip, rocky road.)

✓ Which toppings would you choose if you were ordering a pizza? You may choose as many as you would order on one pizza. (Give students a choice from 10 popular toppings: cheese, pepperoni, chicken, sausage, ham, ground beef, mushrooms, green pepper, pineapple, onions.)

✓ What kind of music do you listen to most often? (Give students the choice of classic rock and roll, rap, hip hop, top forty, country, alternative rock, classical, or "I don't listen to music.")

✓ Another topic of your own choice, approved by your teacher.

Once you have chosen your topic, design a way to organize your data. When the data has been collected, construct a bar graph to display the results of your survey. Generate this graph using a computer program or design it on graph paper. Label each axis and give your graph a title. Compose two paragraphs, one describing your experience conducting the survey and the other analyzing the results. Include in the second paragraph conclusions that can be drawn from the data concerning the students in your school.

Closure: Display the students' graphs in the classroom. Students within each tier can compare and contrast their data, looking for any patterns that might emerge. They can also share their written interpretations of their graphs.

Math Application Problems

Overview: *These tiered assignments allow students to apply mathematical concepts and skills to real-life problems. The word problems at each tier enable students to make decisions about how to set up a problem and provide practice in determining which math algorithm, skill, or concept is needed to solve the problem.* Introduce students to a variety of problem solving strategies prior to attempting these tasks. Students work independently or with a partner to solve each problem. Assign students to the appropriate tier based upon their ability to read and interpret what is needed to solve math application problems.

Standards:
- ➢ Make decisions about how to approach a math application problem
- ➢ Use strategies, skills, and concepts in finding solutions to math application problems
- ➢ Justify the reasoning used to solve math application problems

Objectives:

The students will **KNOW**
- When and how to break a problem into simpler parts.
- The method of deriving the solution to a particular math application problem can assist in solving problems in other situations.

The students will **UNDERSTAND THAT**
- Strategies and results from simpler math word problems can be applied to more complex problems.
- The validity of the results from a math application problem can be checked based on the context of the problem.

The students will **BE ABLE TO**
- Determine the approach, materials, and strategies to use in solving math word problems.
- Defend the reasoning used and justify the procedures selected to solve math application problems.
- Use a variety of methods to explain mathematical reasoning.

Materials:
- Copies of the math application problems for each tier provided in this lesson
- Paper and pencils

Tier One (lower readiness)

Your teacher will give you word problems to be solved during class today. You may choose to solve them alone or with a partner.

Tier Two (higher readiness)

Your teacher will give you word problems to be solved during class today. You may choose to solve them alone or with a partner.

Closure: Students within each tier share and compare the methods that they used to solve each problem. When students choose different approaches to determine an answer, they can check each other's work to validate whether the answer makes sense within the parameters of the problem. Students in Tier Two can also share their written explanations for each problem.

Worksheet for Tier One

Choose a strategy to solve each of the problems below. Write down the strategy you choose and then solve the problem.

Possible strategies to solve the problems:

Draw a picture

Use addition or subtraction

Make a chart or list

Act it out

Guess and check

Problem 1: Tom had 45 marbles. He gave 14 marbles to Dan. How many marbles did he have left?

Strategy:

Solution:

Problem 2: Mrs. Jones had 33 crayons. Her students broke 18 of the crayons. How many crayons were not broken?

Strategy:

Solution:

Problem 3: The Nature Museum had a display of insects. There were 25 beetles, 11 butterflies, 32 crickets, and 2 cockroaches. How many insects did the museum have on display?

Strategy:

Solution:

Problem 4: Bill had 150 baseball cards. He gave 35 of his cards to his little brother for a birthday present. How many cards did Bill have left?

Strategy:

Solution:

Problem 5: Mr. Harrison had 50 pieces of Jolly Ranchers© candy. He gave exactly 5 pieces of candy to each student in one of his reading groups, and none were left over. How many students were in that reading group?

Strategy:

Solution:

Problem 6: Mr. Edward's class was having a pizza party. He ordered four pizzas. Each pizza had 8 slices. How many pieces of pizza were there all together?

Strategy:

Solution:

Problem 7: Betsy needed food for her pet rabbit. Her mother took her to the pet store, and they bought five bags of rabbit food. Each bag cost $8.00. How much money did Betsy spend on rabbit food?

Strategy:

Solution:

Problem 8: Harry Potter's team scored 40 points in the first half of the quiddich match. In the second half, Harry's team scored 30 points. The other team, the Hufflepuffs, scored 50 points during the whole game. Who won the game? How many points did the winning team have?

Strategy:

Solution:

Worksheet for Tier Two

For each of the word problems written below, decide on a way to solve the problem. Will you draw a picture? Use addition, subtraction, multiplication, or division? Make a chart? Guess and check? You decide which method to use. After you solve the problem, write several sentences explaining how you found the answer.

Problem 1: Mrs. Walters' class needs 150 napkins for a party. A small package of 50 napkins costs $0.99. A large package of 150 napkins costs $2.75. How much money would Mrs. Walters save if she bought the package of 150 napkins?

SOLUTION:

WRITTEN EXPLANATION:

Problem 2: John is helping his father box up used golf balls for a special sale at his father's store. Each box will hold 6 golf balls. The cost of one box is $4.00. How many boxes will they need to box up 52 golf balls?

SOLUTION:

WRITTEN EXPLANATION:

Problem 3: There were 4 frogs on each lily pad in a pond that had 8 lily pads. There were 3 ducks swimming around each lily pad. How many more frogs than ducks were there in the pond?

SOLUTION:

WRITTEN EXPLANATION:

Problem 4: Zach wanted to give 4 boxes of Nerds© to every guest at his party. There were 9 boys at his party. Three of the boys ate 2 boxes of their Nerds at the party. One boy ate 3 of his boxes. The rest of the boys ate all of their boxes of Nerds. How many boxes of Nerds were eaten at the party?

SOLUTION:

WRITTEN EXPLANATION:

Problem 5: One summer Jim kept a record of how many kilometers he rode on his skateboard. He won't tell how far he rode, but he will give you these clues:

- It is less than 100.
- It is more than 44.
- If you count by 4s, you say the number's name.
- The number can be divided evenly by 5 and 8.

How many kilometers did Jim travel on his skateboard?

SOLUTION:

WRITTEN EXPLANATION:

Problem 6: Melody and Mandy are circus elephants. They always lead the circus parade. Melody is 4 years old, and Mandy is 13 years old. When will Mandy be twice as old as Melody?

SOLUTION:

WRITTEN EXPLANATION:

Problem 7: At the State Fair, Mark is throwing balls at bowling pins and bottles. He gets 5 points for every bowling pin he hits and 8 points for every bottle he hits. He can win a big stuffed bear by earning 100 points. Mark has hit 13 bowling pins and bottles all together and has earned 80 points. How many bowling pins and how many bottles did he hit to reach 80 points?

SOLUTION:

WRITTEN EXPLANATION:

Problem 8: Neal and Rhoda are going to Mallory's Department Store to get their picture taken. There are four different doors into the store. There is one escalator, one stairway, or two elevators that they can take to the third floor where the photographer is. Once on the third floor, there are two different doors into the photographer's studio. How many ways can Neal and Rhoda go from outside the store to the photographer's studio on the third floor?

SOLUTION:

WRITTEN EXPLANATION:

Measurement of Length, Area, and Volume

Overview: *These tiered activities provide students with the opportunity to apply their knowledge of the U.S. customary and metric systems of measurement to real-life situations.* Prior to assigning these tasks, read the math picture book Counting on Frank by Rod Clement to the whole class. Many school and community libraries have this book in their collections, and it is available for purchase at a variety of web sites. Use Counting on Frank as a model for the class to create its original book entitled Counting on (Mount Union School), substituting the students' own school name.

Standards:
> ➢ Differentiate between length/perimeter, area, and volume, and identify whether the application of the concept of length/perimeter, area, or volume is appropriate for a given situation
> ➢ Choose an appropriate measuring device and unit of measure to solve problems involving measurement of length, area, and volume

Objectives:

The students will **KNOW**
- *Perimeter* is the distance around an object and is a measure of length.
- *Area* is the number of square units needed to cover a surface.
- *Volume* is a measure of capacity.

The students will **UNDERSTAND THAT**
- There is a difference between using perimeter, area, and volume in a given situation.
- The context of the measurement problem will determine which unit is appropriate for expressing the measured value.
- Calculating and describing measurements is a life skill that is pervasive and on going in the real world.

The students will **BE ABLE TO**
- Name standard and metric units of measure for length, weight/mass, and volume.
- Analyze a measurement problem to determine the appropriate unit of measure to use.
- Solve problems involving measurement by selecting an appropriate measuring device and a U.S. customary or metric unit of measure.
- Describe real-life situations where perimeter, area, and volume are appropriate measures to use and justify choices in writing.

Materials:
- A copy of the math picture book Counting on Frank by Rod Clement
- Assorted art materials to create the pages of the class book
- Measurement tools (rulers, yardsticks, tape measures) as needed depending upon the problem selected
- Calculators

(Note: The goal of these tasks at all three levels is to complete a class measurement book modeled after the content and format of Counting on Frank. Give students the option of working alone or with a partner to create a page for the book. Once the students have selected the topics for their pages, they create the text and design the book's format. The teacher chooses the type and size of paper for the pages of the book, whether the text should be handwritten or generated on the word processor by the students, and the medium to use for illustrations. All tiers will need instruction from the teacher once these decisions have been made. Once their pages have been completed, the students must describe in a paragraph on a separate piece of paper how their problem was solved as well as any calculations that were needed to solve it. These solutions can be assembled together in the back of the book. Explain all of these decisions and processes to the whole class before specific instructions are given to each tier. It is suggested that the book's pages be laminated before binding.)

Tier One (lower readiness)

You may choose to work alone or with a partner to complete these tasks. After your teacher has read the book Counting on Frank, your first job is to create a measurement problem based on *length* that involves a situation around your classroom or school. You may choose to build your problem around either distance or perimeter. For example, the building manager stacks chairs in the cafeteria. On your page in the book show how many days it would take the column of chairs to reach the ceiling of the cafeteria, stacking one chair each day. The building manager can find out the height of the room's ceiling for you.

Now, design your own problem. Next, you must figure out how to solve this problem and create a clever way of describing it and showing the answer on your page of the book. Illustrate your problem, and end the page with a humorous statement, as each problem does in Counting on Frank. Your last task is to use a separate piece of paper to describe how you solved the problem, and show any calculations that you made to get the answer. You may use a calculator. Whatever subject you choose for your problem, you will have to make some measurements to find the solution.

Tier Two (middle readiness)

You may choose to work alone or with a partner to complete these tasks. After your teacher has read the book Counting on Frank, your first job is to create a measurement problem based on *area* that involves a situation around your classroom or school. For example, suppose that students have been dropping food on the floor during snack time, and your teacher is getting upset. Imagine a Pringle's© potato chip was dropped every day. How many days would it take to cover the floor of your classroom with Pringle's© chips? The potato chip is not a standard shape. To approximate its area, use a ruler to draw the smallest possible rectangle around the chip, measure the rectangle's length and width, and calculate that area. Using this method, you can work with irregularly shaped objects.

Now, design your own problem. Next, you must figure out how to solve the problem, and create a clever way of describing it and showing the answer on your page of the book. Illustrate your problem, and end the page with a humorous statement, as each problem does in Counting on Frank. Your last task is to use a separate piece of paper to describe how you solved the problem and show any calculations that you made to get the answer. You may use a calculator. Whatever subject you choose for your problem, you have to make some measurements to find the solution.

Tier Three (higher readiness)

You may choose to work alone or with a partner to complete these tasks. After your teacher has read the book Counting on Frank, your first job is to create a measurement problem based on *volume* that involves a situation around your classroom or school. For example, suppose a student collected pencils. If one pencil a day were placed inside an empty desk in your classroom, how many days would it take to fill the desk with pencils? In order to solve this problem, you need to know the volume of the pencil, which is not a regular geometric shape. To approximate the volume of the pencil, measure the length, width, and height of the smallest possible rectangular prism (box) that would fit around the pencil. In the book, this is how the boy determined how many Frank's would fit into his room. He scrunched Frank up into a small heap and measured the smallest possible rectangular prism that fit around Frank.

Now, design your own problem. Next, you must figure out how to solve this problem, and create a clever way of describing it and showing the answer on your page of the book. Illustrate your problem, and end the page with a humorous statement, as each problem does in Counting on Frank. Your last task is to use a separate piece of paper to describe how you solved the problem, and show any calculations that you made to get the answer. You may use a calculator. Whatever subject you choose for your problem, you have to make some measurements to find the solution.

Closure: Compile all the pages of Counting on *(the name of your school)* into a book bound in the manner of your choice. Read and show the class book to the students. Allow students to discuss in small, mixed-readiness groups how they chose their problems, what they had to do to solve them, and any humorous or unusual incidences that occurred while they were measuring, etc. Place the completed book in the school media center to share with the whole school.

Money

Overview: *These tiered assignments give students the opportunity to practice counting money and to apply their knowledge of the relationships that exist between coins and bills in the United States monetary system.* Each tier explains how to group students to accomplish the given tasks. Assign students to tiers based upon their level of understanding of our system of money and their need for concrete versus abstract activities.

Standards:
  ➢ Count and compare a collection of pennies, nickels, dimes, and quarters
  ➢ Identify the correct usage of the cent symbol (¢), dollar symbol ($), and decimal point (.)
  ➢ Determine by counting the value of a collection of bills and coins, compare the value of the coins or bills, and make change
  ➢ Solve problems that involve amounts of money

Objectives:
The students will **KNOW**
  • The money system in the United States consists of coins and bills based on ones, fives, and tens, making it easy to count money.
  • The *dollar* is the basic unit of exchange.
  • Money can be counted by grouping coins and bills to determine the value of each group and then adding to determine the total value.

The students will **UNDERSTAND THAT**
  • The appropriate number of pennies, nickels, dimes, and quarters can be exchanged for a different combination of coins that equal an equivalent amount.
  • Money amounts are meaningless unless the cent symbol, dollar symbol, and decimal point are used correctly.
  • Counting money helps a student gain an awareness of consumer skills and the use of money in everyday life.

The students will **BE ABLE TO**
  • Identify the value of a nickel, a dime, and a quarter in terms of pennies.
  • Recognize the physical characteristics of pennies, nickels, dimes, and quarters.
  • Identify the value of a collection of coins.
  • Simulate everyday opportunities to count and compare collections of coins and bills.
  • Make change.
  • Shop for a collection of items when given a maximum amount to spend.

Materials:

Tier One

❖ Either a teacher-made or a commercial worksheet showing food items to purchase and their cost, empty cans and boxes of food products with the cost labeled, or a newspaper grocery store ad that indicates a variety of food items to purchase and the cost of each

❖ Collections of pennies, nickels, dimes, and quarters that equal an amount determined by the teacher

Tier Two

❖ Collections of random amounts of pennies, nickels, dimes, quarters, and dollar bills

Tier Three

❖ A collection of different catalogues selling appropriate items for students to purchase

Tier One (lower readiness)

Students at this tier count collections of coins and purchase food items with the amount they have to spend. Students work with a partner to complete the tasks. Each student is given a collection of pennies, nickels, dimes, and quarters to equal $5.00, or any other amount determined by the teacher. Students will also be given one of the following collections of food items:

✓ A teacher-made or a commercial worksheet showing food items to purchase and their cost

✓ Empty cans and boxes of food products with the cost labeled

✓ A newspaper grocery store ad that indicates a variety of food items to purchase and the cost of each

Working in pairs, students take turns playing the role of the shopper and the grocer.

One student shops to purchase as much food as possible without going over the value of his/her collection of coins, paying the grocer for each item as it is bought. The grocer then determines how much, if any, change the shopper receives. Partners then reverse roles. The students may shop more than once to buy a different collection of food for as long as time permits.

Tier Two (middle readiness)

Give students at this tier a random amount of coins and bills. The first task is for each student to count the amount of money that was received. The second task is for each person to find a student within Tier Two whose collection of money comes closest to equaling the amount that he/she was given. The entire tier has to work collaboratively to match members with the closest values. Next, the matched pairs determine the difference between the amounts of money each paired student possesses. The two students with the least difference between their amounts, zero being the optimum, win that round. Distribute a second random collection of money so that another round can be played. Or, one student can play the role of banker. Everyone turns in all money to the banker, and that person randomly passes collections of coins and bills back to the members of the tier. The activity begins over again, with the counting of money, finding a partner with the closest amount, and determining the difference between amounts. It is important that the random money amounts given during each round of play change between rounds.

Tier Three (higher readiness)

Students go on a shopping spree using a catalogue for purchase choices. The teacher can collect a variety of catalogues or ask students to bring them from home if available and if selling appropriate goods. Toy catalogues are perfect, but any appropriate catalogue works. Give each student a certain amount of money to spend on catalogue items. The total is up to the teacher's discretion, depending upon how large an amount the students can effectively handle. This tier does not receive actual coins and bills, but works with the values abstractly. If the given value is $100.00, each student selects the items he/she wishes to purchase, with the total getting as close to $100.00 as possible without going over $100.00. The next task is to calculate how much change will be received after purchasing the goods. Students can then trade catalogues with another member of the tier, the teacher can assign a different value with which to shop, and the activity begins over again.

Closure: Students in *Tier One* and *Tier Three* can share within their tiers their purchase lists and how close they came to spending all of their money. Students in *Tier Two* can share the strategies they used to find someone whose money value was closest to their own. The teacher brings all tiers back together to pose the following questions:
- What happens when we don't have enough money to buy what we want?
- What is the quickest way to count a collection of coins and bills?
- Do we really need pennies in our money system?

Polyhedrons/3-Dimensional Figures

Overview: *These tiered assignments provide students with the opportunity to solidify their grasp of polyhedrons and to practice creating polyhedrons.* Before working on their assigned tasks, introduce students to the names, characteristics, and parts of a variety of polyhedrons. Complete the following introductory activities as a whole group or in smaller, randomly-assigned groups:

❖ Students explore a variety of 3-dimensional figures as the teacher introduces the term *polyhedron* (many-sided). How are these figures alike? Different?

❖ Students identify objects in the classroom that represent the polyhedrons they have examined. This can be accomplished through a "Polyhedron Hunt."

❖ Introduce the parts of common polyhedrons (base, face, edge, vertex) and identify these parts on models of polyhedrons.

❖ Play a polyhedron guessing game. In this game, blindfold students and give them a polyhedron to hold and feel. What is the name of the polyhedron? What parts can they feel?

Standards:
➢ Recognize the attributes of three-dimensional geometric figures
➢ Describe and make solid figures

Objectives:
The students will **KNOW**
• Names of common polyhedrons (cube, prism, sphere, cylinder, cone, pyramid).
• Names of the parts of polyhedrons ((base, face, edge, vertex).
The students will **UNDERSTAND THAT**
• Geometric figures can be described and named based on their characteristics/parts.
• We can find geometric figures all around us.
The students will **BE ABLE TO**
• Describe polyhedrons.
• Identify the parts of polyhedrons.
• Create polyhedrons.

Materials:
• Pattern blocks
• Models of a variety of polyhedrons
• Straws (cut into short segments) and twist ties

Tier One (lower readiness)

Students working on this tier work in pairs to create a variety of polyhedrons by stacking pattern blocks. As they work, they ask one another to guess which polyhedrons they have made. Encourage them to make the same polyhedrons in different ways by using different pattern blocks and by combining pattern blocks to create different bases for their polyhedrons.

After they have created several different polyhedrons with the pattern blocks, they remain in their pairs to play a reverse guessing game. One student secretly selects a polyhedron model and describes it to the other student who cannot see it. The second student will try to guess the name of the polyhedron based on the information provided. The pairs can play this game several times, taking turns as they go.

Tier Two (higher readiness)

Students in this group work independently to create some of the polyhedrons studied using straws and twist ties (the twist ties connect two straws and can be bent to create vertices). What polyhedron parts do the straws and twist ties represent? Have students create signs/labels for the polyhedrons they create, and display their polyhedrons.

After the students have created two to three common polyhedrons (depending on the pace at which they are able to work with the straws and twist ties), they use straws and twist ties to create original polyhedrons. Have them name their polyhedrons based on their characteristics. For example, a four-sided figure with one base could be named a "quadripyramid" based on its number of bases and faces. Have the students create signs/labels for their creations.

Closure: After the students have completed their tasks, review the term *polyhedron* as well as the names and the parts of common polyhedrons. Additional questions for discussion include:
- What is your favorite polyhedron? Why?
- Which polyhedron is the most important? Why?
- Is a sphere a polyhedron? Why or why not?

Readiness-Based
Science
Tiered Assignments

The Interdependence of Plants and Animals

Overview: *These tiered activities give students an opportunity to apply their understandings of the flow of energy through food chains within any given ecosystem.* At each of the two tiers, students investigate and describe the interdependent relationships that exist between plants and animals in an ecosystem. Have students complete these activities after they have studied the structure of food chains and the functions of organisms within the population of the ecosystem. Assign students to the appropriate activities based on the students' grasp of the interdependence of plants and animals, as well as on the students' abilities to work successfully with independent tasks.

Standards:
➤ Investigate and understand relationships among organisms in food chains
➤ Understand that all organisms need energy and matter to live and grow
➤ Build an understanding of the interdependence of plants and animals

Objectives:
The students will **KNOW**
• An animal that hunts other animals to get its food is a *predator*.
• An animal that can be hunted by another animal for food is a *prey*.
• Green plants are *producers*; they make their own food from sunlight, air, and water.
• Animals are *consumers* because they eat living organisms, plant and/or animal.
• *Decomposers* are organisms that break down decayed plants and animals into smaller pieces that can be used again by living things.
• The organization of communities is based on the use of the energy from the sun within a given ecosystem.

The students will **UNDERSTAND THAT**

- A food chain shows a food relationship among plants and animals in a specific ecosystem or environment.
- The sun's energy cycles through ecosystems from producers through consumers and back into the nutrient pool through decomposers.
- The greatest amount of energy in an ecosystem is in the producers.
- A food chain shows a food relationship among plants and animals in a specific ecosystem or environment.

The students will **BE ABLE TO**

- Distinguish among producers, consumers, and decomposers.
- Create and interpret a model of a food chain.
- Differentiate between predators and prey.
- Infer that most food chains begin with a green plant.
- Work independently and cooperatively.

Materials:

- A variety of pictures of plants and animals indigenous to given ecosystems, obtained from magazines, old textbooks, calendars, and/or the Internet
- Scissors and glue
- Construction paper or tag board
- A wooden log that has not begun decomposition
- A decaying log retrieved from a natural setting
- Magnifying glasses
- Microscope (if available)
- Access to the Internet

(Note: It will probably take two days of class time to complete the activities in both of these tiers.)

Closure: When the students have completed their products, place them into small, mixed-readiness groups to share their work and learning. After adequate time has been provided for discussion in these small groups, the students come together as a whole class to discuss the following questions:

- What is the most important thing to know about the interdependence of plants and animals?
- What is an example of a food web that humans are part of?
- What is a new idea that you learned today that you think is important for us to understand?
- What would happen to us if there were no green plants?

Tier One (lower readiness)

Students working at this tier have the option of working in pairs or working independently to complete the following tasks:

1) The students examine a collection of pictures of plants and animals indigenous to the ecosystems that have been studied in class. The teacher has the option of collecting these pictures from magazines, calendars, the Internet, etc., or the students can find the pictures on their own by searching the Web, magazines, or other resources provided by the teacher.

2) Students then categorize these pictures in the following ways. They may use reference materials, their science text, or the Internet as resources as needed.
    a. Producers and consumers
    b. Living things that get their energy directly from the sun and those that do not
    c. Predators and prey

3) As each category is formed, the students list the living things that are included in that category. Next, the students use the pictures to construct a food web that would exist in a particular ecosystem. They glue pictures on construction paper or tag board with arrows drawn to indicate how energy moves through the web.

4) The students examine a rotting log retrieved from a natural environment to observe the effects of decomposers on decaying plants. They can use magnifying glasses to examine the texture and composition of the wood fibers, or small quantities can be placed under a microscope, if available. The students draw or describe in written format what they observe. They also examine a log that has not yet begun the process of decomposition and write a short paragraph to describe the differences between the two logs.

Tier Two (higher readiness)

Students assigned to this tier explore the Worldwide Web to extend their knowledge of the interdependence of plants and animals. A variety of web sites are listed below, many containing multiple links to informational and interactive experiences that further student knowledge of interdependence and food webs/chains. The sites were chosen because they address all of the lesson standards and objectives. Access to the Internet is critical to this tier. Preview all links before sharing them with students to verify that the sites are still active. Students may work either independently or with partners to explore the following websites:

http://www.picadome.fcps.net/lab/currl/food_chain/default.htm

This site offers links to 40 interactive and informational sites that address all of the objectives of this lesson at a variety of grade levels. Students could spend an entire period just exploring this site.

http://www.vtaide.com/png/foodchains.htm

This site offers support information on the levels of a food chain. When students click on the link "Create a Food Web," they are offered a wide variety of plant and animals from which they can design their own web and print it to share with their classmates.

http://www.ers.north-ayrshire.gov.uk/food_chains.htm

This site is sponsored by the BBC and offers activities for both primary and elementary students.

http://www.emints.org/ethemes/resources/S00000328.shtml

This site addresses grades 2-5 and offers links to twenty different web sites that address informational and interactive information about food chains and webs.

http://www.rblewis.net/technology/EDU506/WebQuests/foodchain/foodchain.html

This site is intended for grades 2-4 and leads students through a web quest on food chains.

http://www.lethsd.ab.ca/mmh/grade5/wetlands/page7.htm

This site focuses on wetland food chains, with a variety of links that are interactive and informative. Although it is designed for plants and animals in Canada, the concepts are universal.

http://www.kn.pacbell.com/wired/fil/pages/samfoodchast.html

This site, entitled "Food Chain, an Internet Sampler," gives students links and projects to further their knowledge of food chains.

At the end of the class period, the students pick two sites/activities that they feel most expanded their knowledge of interdependence, and they compose paragraphs explaining what new knowledge they gained from the sites/activities.

Mammals

Overview: *These tiered activities give students an opportunity to apply their understandings of the characteristics of mammals.* At each tier, students work on identifying mammals, describing their characteristics, and explaining where different mammals live. Following readings (for example, <u>Animals Born Alive and Well</u>), class discussions, and if possible, observations of mammals, assign students to the appropriate assignments based on the students' grasp of the unique features of mammals as well as on the students' abilities to work successfully with open-ended tasks.

Standards:
> ➤ Build an understanding of similarities and differences in animals
> ➤ Build an understanding of the needs of living things

Objectives:

The students will **KNOW**
- The characteristics that define mammals (for example, mammals are warm-blooded and generally do not lay eggs).
- Names of many different mammals.
- Places where mammals live.

The students will **UNDERSTAND THAT**
- Animals are divided into different groups based on their characteristics.
- All animals have basic needs that must be met in order for them to survive, and these needs are met in the animals' environments.

The students will **BE ABLE TO**
- Sort animals based on whether or not they are mammals.
- Discuss the characteristics of mammals.
- Show where mammals live.
- Use available resources to answer questions.
- Work independently and cooperatively.

Materials:
- A variety of books about animals and mammals
- Several sets of pictures of different animals (sets must include mammals and non-mammals)
- Copies of *"What Makes a Mammal a Mammal?"* provided in this lesson
- Copies of a map of the world
- Copies of *"About Mammals"* provided in this lesson

- Paper, colored pencils, crayons, markers
- Copies of *"Mammal Research"* provided in this lesson
- Magazines and other print resources that provide pictures of animals

Tier One (lower readiness)

Students working at this tier work in pairs to complete the following tasks. Present these tasks to the learners at one time or as they complete each one.

1) Given a variety of pictures of different animals, the students sort the pictures into two groups: *"Mammals"* and *"Not mammals."* The students use classroom resources as needed. Once they have finished this sorting task, check the students' work and provide feedback as necessary.

2) Then the students work in their pairs to write or dictate 2-3 sentences about mammals on the sheet *"What Makes a Mammal a Mammal?"* They also list or illustrate at least 3 examples of mammals on this sheet. Though the students may share ideas with their partners, have each student complete his or her own sheet.

3) Once the students working at this tier have completed their first task, the teacher gives each student a copy of a map of the world. The students continue working in pairs to write the name of or illustrate at least 2 mammals on each of the continents. It may be necessary to review the continents with the students. Each student creates his or her own map, and the students use classroom resources as needed.

Tier Two (middle readiness)

Students assigned to this tier work either independently or with partners on any of the following tasks.

1) The students brainstorm and list animals that are mammals and animals that are not mammals on the sheet provided *("About Mammals")*. They record at least 8 animals in each list. At the bottom of the sheet, they write at least 3 sentences about the characteristics of mammals.

2) Next, the students create booklets that include the following pages: *"Mammals of the Tundra," "Mammals of the Desert," "Mammals of the Ocean,"* and *"Mammals of the Forest."* While the students may work with a partner to generate ideas for their booklets, each student must create his or her own booklet by writing and drawing on each page. Their writing should address how the mammals that live in each environment are able to survive. For example, how can polar bears survive in the tundra?

Tier Three (higher readiness)

Students working at this tier conduct independent research about a mammal of their choice using the *"Mammal Research"* sheets provided. They use classroom resources as needed and may require assistance with finding additional resources. Each student selects one mammal to research and provides the following information about it: what makes it a mammal, where it lives, why it can survive where it lives, what it eats, and some interesting information about the mammal. The students also provide illustrations of their mammals that show the characteristics of the mammals as well as where they live (these can be student created or found in magazines or other resources). Encourage the students working at this tier to research mammals that are unfamiliar to them.

Closure: Show a picture of or name an animal that is not a mammal. Ask the students whether or not it is a mammal, and invite them to explain why it is or is not. On the board or an overhead, create a class acrostic using the word "mammal." Use Think-Pair-Share to encourage students to share their ideas with a classmate before sharing them with the whole group.

What Makes a Mammal a Mammal?

Here are some characteristics of mammals:

_____

_____

_____

_____

_____

_____

_____

Here are some mammals:

© Pieces of Learning

About Mammals

Mammals   **Not Mammals**

Here are some characteristics of mammals:

_____

_____

_____

_____

_____

_____

_____

Mammal Research

The mammal I am researching is the _____

This animal is a mammal because _____

_____

_____

_____

_____

_____

It lives in _____

_____

It can survive here because _____

_____

_____

It eats _____

_____

_____

Here are some unique characteristics of my mammal:

_____

_____

_____

_____

_____

The Hydrosphere and Its Water Cycle

Overview: *These tiered activities give students an opportunity to apply their understandings of the water cycle and the value of water as a natural resource.* At each tier, students illustrate and/or explain either the water cycle or the importance of conserving water. Have students complete these activities after the class has studied the water cycle and the role water plays in our survival as a species. Assign students to the appropriate activities based on the students' understanding of the water cycle, as well as on the students' abilities to work successfully with open-ended tasks.

Standards:
 ➤ Investigate and understand the water cycle and its relationship to life on Earth
 ➤ Examine the finite nature of water as a limited resource and determine ways to conserve and protect it.

Objectives:

The students will **KNOW**
 • The *water cycle* is the movement of water from the ground to the air and back to the ground by evaporation, condensation, and precipitation.
 • Most of the Earth's water is present as salt water in the oceans.
 • The origin of the water used by their local communities.

The students will **UNDERSTAND THAT**
 • The sun provides the energy that drives the water cycle.
 • Pollution reduces the amount of usable fresh water; therefore the supply should be conserved carefully.
 • The amount of fresh water located in rivers, lakes, underground sources, and glaciers is limited and that its availability can be extended by recycling and decreasing the use of water.
 • Water is a simple compound essential for life on Earth.

The students will **BE ABLE TO**
 • Identify the sun as the origin of energy that drives the water cycle.
 • Describe the processes of evaporation, condensation, and precipitation as they relate to the water cycle.
 • Identify major water sources for the local communities.
 • Explain methods of water conservation in the home and the school.
 • Explain the importance of water to people and other living things.

Materials:

Tier One

- Large, zip-lock® plastic baggies
- Water
- Food coloring
- Masking tape
- Thermometer
- Colored ice cubes

Tier Two

- Copies of world maps or an atlas
- Art supplies for illustrations

Tier Three

- Poster board
- Markers, crayons, or colored pencils
- Calculators
- Internet access

Closure: This lesson provides the opportunity for students working at each tier to share their products with the whole class. If time does not permit, the students can share their products within their tiers (similar-readiness groups), and then these groups can pick one product from the tier to be shared with the whole class.

Tier One (lower readiness)

Students working at this tier have the option of working in pairs or working independently to complete the following tasks:

1) Students build a simple model of the water cycle to illustrate its effectiveness to the rest of the class. The procedure for constructing the model is as follows:
   a. Put about a cup of water into a plastic baggie.
   b. Add two drops of food coloring.
   c. Carefully seal the baggie, and use the masking tape to tape it onto a sunny window. Use enough tape to hold the bag securely. If the heat is on in that classroom and there is a window over the heater, tape the bag to the window.
   d. Hold the bulb of the thermometer against the bag for three minutes, and then record the temperature.
   e. Let the bag hang in the sun for several hours, and then observe it carefully. Look for any changes in the bag. Hold the bulb of the thermometer against the bag again for three minutes. Record any change in temperature.

2) Students answer the following questions after observing the bag the second time.
   a. From where did the tiny droplets of water on the side of the bag come?
   b. Can you tell if there is any less water in the bottom of the bag? How would you find out?
   c. Hold a piece of colored ice against the condensed water vapor inside the bag. What happens?

3) Move the bag to a location where there is no sun, and tape it there for several hours. How does this new location affect the water cycle?

4) Compose a paragraph explaining how your demonstration modeled the real water cycle. Draw a diagram to help with your explanation.

Tier Two (middle readiness)

Students assigned to this tier work either independently or with partners to complete the tasks outlined below.

Student information needed to complete this tier: Earth's water is always in movement, and the water cycle describes the continuous movement of water on, above, and below the surface of the Earth. Since the water cycle is truly a "cycle," there is no beginning or end. Water can change states among liquid, vapor, and ice at various places in the water cycle, with these processes happening in the blink of an eye and/or over millions of years.

The water in the apple you ate yesterday may have fallen as rain halfway around the world last year or could have been used 100 million years ago by Mama Dinosaur to give her baby a bath. A drop of water can move back and forth between the following forms and locations: rain, snow, sleet, hail, clouds, fog, oceans, lakes, rivers, swamps, sounds, glaciers, ice bergs, puddles, and runoff from paved roads and surfaces.

Students become a drop of water in its journey through the water cycle for one year and compose a travel journal/diary describing this journey. The water droplet can begin and end at the location of the students' choice. Students assume the role of the drop of water and write from its point of view. They may add illustrations to their journal if they choose. They may select as many forms as they would like to take in their yearlong journey.

Questions to consider:
- ✓ How does it feel to change from liquid water, to water vapor or ice, and back to liquid water again?
- ✓ Where do you travel (use a world map as needed) and what forms of water do you take as you evaporate and condense?
- ✓ How long do you stay in the clouds, the ocean, or wherever you find yourself?

Tier Three (higher readiness)

Students assigned to this tier identify water sources within their communities and investigate how to conserve water. They may work either independently or with partners to complete the following tasks:

1) The students first contact the local city or county water department to determine the source or sources of fresh water for the local communities. If living outside a town or city, they also collect data on what percentage of households use wells, if this information is available. Students then construct a map or chart to inform the rest of the class where fresh water is obtained in the community.

2) Students next calculate how much water their households use per day. The average amount of water involved in the following daily activities is approximately:

   - 5 gal. Flushing a toilet
   - 25 gal. Taking a short shower
   - 35 gal. Taking a tub bath
   - 2 gal. Brushing teeth
   - 30 gal. Washing dishes with the water running
   - 10 gal. Washing dishes in a basin or sink
   - 20 gal. Using the dishwasher
   - 35 gal. Using a washing machine

   Multiply the amount of water you use for each activity above by the number of times each day you do it. Then multiply that figure by the number of people in your household. You may use a calculator. How much water did your family use today?

3) For their final task, students create a plan to reduce the amount of water used by their families. Research water conservation on the Internet for suggestions that will work for the local households in the community. Students may also create new conservation measures of their own. The plan can be written as a report or displayed on poster board.

Parts of Flowers

Overview: *These readiness-based tasks give students a chance to identify the parts of flowers while working at appropriate levels of challenge.* The students work independently on these tasks following whole-group activities designed to introduce the role of flowers in plant life and the parts of flowers, such as:

- ❖ Reading The Reason for a Flower by Ruth Heller
- ❖ Examining simple flowers such as lilies and looking for and exploring their parts

Assign students to the tiered tasks below based on both teacher observation of their grasp of flower parts during introductory activities and on the students' writing abilities. These tasks can be used as assessment of the students' abilities to identify flower parts.

Standard:

➢ Observe and describe the parts of plants

Objectives:

The students will **KNOW**

- Plant parts (root, stem, leaf, flower).
- Flowers parts (petal, pistil, stigma, style, ovary, stamen, anther, filament).

The students will **UNDERSTAND THAT**

- Flowers, like plants, are made up of different parts, and each part has a job to do.
- Through careful observation, we can learn about the world around us.

The students will **BE ABLE TO**

- Make observations.
- Identify and label flower parts.
- Compare and contrast.

Materials:

- Large pictures of flowers from magazines, catalogs, or calendars (make sure that the parts of the flowers can be seen)
- Stickers showing names of flower parts
- Paper, pencils, crayons, markers
- Books showing different flowers

Closure: As a whole group, the students share their work and review the parts of flowers. What is the job of a flower? How does a flower help a plant? Why are the parts of flowers important?

Tier One (lower readiness)

Students working at this tier identify flower parts on pictures provided in the classroom. The students label the parts using stickers that show the names of the parts. When they have identified and labeled as many parts as they can, they work with another student assigned to this tier to compare and contrast 2-3 pictures of flowers and their parts. How are flower parts similar and different in different types of flowers?

Tier Two (higher readiness)

Students assigned to this tier create and label pictures of flowers making sure to show and label the parts of the flowers. They use classroom resources as needed to help them create realistic illustrations. When they have completed their labeled illustrations, they work with a partner to share their work and to identify the similarities and differences between their flowers and the parts of their flowers.

Weathering and Erosion

<u>**Overview**</u>: *These tiered activities give students an opportunity to apply their understandings of the effects that weathering and erosion have on the Earth's surface*. At each tier, students illustrate and/or explain the process that changes the structure of the landscape. Have students complete these activities after the class has studied the causes and effects of weathering and erosion. Assign students to the appropriate activities based on the students' grasp of the geological processes, as well as on the students' abilities to work successfully with open-ended tasks.

Standards:
➢ Investigate and understand how the Earth's surface is constantly changing
➢ Discuss the properties of rocks and minerals and the processes that formed them
➢ Build an understanding of solid earth materials

Objectives:

The students will **KNOW**

- Some changes to the Earth's surface are due to slow processes, such as erosion, and some changes are due to rapid processes, such as landslides, volcanic eruptions, and earthquakes.
- Moving water erodes landforms, reshaping the land by taking it away from some places and depositing it as pebbles, sand, silt, and mud in other places.
- The products of weathering include clay, sand, rock fragments, and soluble substances.

The students will **UNDERSTAND THAT**

- Smaller rocks come from the breakage and weathering of larger rocks.
- Rocks and minerals on the Earth's surface are constantly being broken down both chemically and physically.
- Weathered rock material can be moved by water and wind and deposited as sediment.

The students will **BE ABLE TO**

- Identify and analyze forces that cause change in landforms over time.
- Describe the deposition of eroded material and its importance in establishing landforms.
- Differentiate between weathering and erosion.
- Compare and contrast scientific concepts.
- Work independently and cooperatively.

Materials:
- A variety of books on weathering and erosion
- Internet availability
- A variety of pictures/images that illustrate examples of weathering, erosion, and diverse landforms. These can come from National Geographic, other science-related magazines, or images downloaded from the Internet. Students can search for images on-line.
- Poster board or tag board for collages and displays
- Disposable camera, digital camera, or video camera, if available
- Art materials for students drawing their own images

Closure: When the students have completed their work, provide time for them to share their products either in small groups or with the whole class. Then pose the following questions to the whole group:
- What are some of the primary results of weathering and erosion? Are these positive or negative results? Why?
- In what ways can we control weathering and erosion? Should we control them? Why or why not?

Tier One (lower readiness)

Students working at this tier have the option of working in pairs or working independently to complete the following tasks:

1) Given a variety of pictures of the Earth's surface from several continents, as well as pictures of different landforms, students sort the pictures into two groups: "Examples of Weathering" and "Examples of Erosion." The students use classroom resources as needed to distinguish between the two. Once they have finished this sorting task, check the students' work and provide feedback as needed.

2) Students then use their images to create two collages, one illustrating the effects of weathering and one illustrating the effects of erosion. The number of images available for use determines the size of the collages. Students may also draw their own examples if they wish.

---

3) Once the collages are completed, students compose a paragraph as a caption for each collage. The paragraphs explain erosion and weathering and describe how the collage illustrates each.

Tier Two (middle readiness)

Students assigned to this tier work either independently or with partners to complete the following tasks:

(Note: You may determine the minimum number of sites that students must locate.)

1) Students design an investigation to locate, describe, and report on examples of natural erosion and weathering found in the local community. Students survey the environment around the school grounds or the neighborhood around their homes to find these examples. The descriptions can be documented using cameras, video cameras, or written paragraphs. Have students include the location of the weathering or erosion, the effects on the environment, and a hypothesis regarding what may have caused the weathering or erosion.

2) Next, students choose one of the sites located above and create a plan to solve the erosion or weathering problems that were discovered. Have students include a summary of this plan with the documentation from the first task.

Tier Three (higher readiness)

Students assigned to this tier compare and contrast the natural effects of weathering and erosion with those caused by human changes to the Earth's surface. They work either independently or with partners to complete the following tasks:

1) Students first research the many ways in which people change the Earth's surface to cause weathering and erosion that would not otherwise occur. Reference materials and the Internet provide a variety of examples of man-made erosion and weathering practices.

2) After the completion of the research, students locate a site within the local community where erosion and weathering are occurring only because of human interference with the Earth's surface. If students do not know of a site from personal observation, the local newspaper, library reference center, or environmental groups can assist in providing examples. Ideally, once a site has been selected, have students (or at least one student) visit the site to document with photographs, video, or written description the effects of the man-made erosion. *The teacher or other school personnel might assist with this site visit.* If a student visit cannot occur, an adult who has knowledge of the site can report to the students.

3) Finally, students design a plan that controls or reverses the negative changes to the Earth's surface created by man. Have students include in the plan specific examples of how the community can affect positive change to the site.

Readiness-Based Social Studies Tiered Assignments

Families

<u>Overview</u>: *These tiered activities provide students with the opportunity to explore the lives of actual people who make a difference in the students' day-to-day existence.* These assignments follow classroom lessons about the structure and purpose of family life and the different roles family members assume. Assign the tasks based on students' participation and work during lessons that focus on the family. Have students complete the activities at all three tiers as individual work.

Standards:
- ➢ Analyze how individuals, families, and groups are similar and different
- ➢ Compare and contrast students' daily lives with those of their parents, grandparents, and/or guardians
- ➢ Trace the history of a family through the use of primary and secondary sources, including artifacts, photographs, interviews, and documents

Objectives:

The students will **KNOW**
- • Families can be composed of different types of relationships.
- • Families have many things in common, but each family is different from all others in unique ways.
- • Individual roles differ from one family to another.

The students will **UNDERSTAND THAT**
- • Their family is unique from all others.
- • Their family's history helps to define who they are as individuals.
- • The family is a basic unit of a community.

The students will **BE ABLE TO**
- • Differentiate between things that happened long ago and things that happened recently.
- • Describe the roles of individuals in the family.
- • Compare and contrast similarities and differences among individuals and families.
- • Describe the history of their family.

Materials:
- Drawing paper
- Markers or crayons
- Scissors
- Copies of *"Questions for Interviewing a Member of My Family"* for Tier 2 (provided at the end of this lesson)
- Art supplies to create books and scrapbooks
- Tape recorders, if available and if they can be loaned to students

---

Closure: Each tier finishes with a product. These products can be shared within the members of the tier and then displayed for students in the class to observe and read. Also, when all of the students have completed their products, pose the following questions to the whole group to encourage sharing across the tiers:
- What kinds of things do family members do to help their families?
- Are families the same as they were many years ago? Why or why not? How are they different?
- Do families do the same kinds of things that they did when your parents or grandparents were children?
- How did your parents or grandparents contribute to their families? How do you contribute to your families?
- Why are families important?

Tier One (lower readiness)

Students working at this tier complete the following tasks individually:

1) On a large sheet of drawing paper, draw the outline of your house, apartment, etc. Underneath the drawing, complete the statement, "I live in my house with...." by either writing it or dictating it to someone.

2) Place all of the people who live in your house by either drawing them inside the outline of your home or creating them on construction paper, cutting them out, and gluing them inside the home's outline.

3) Describe the jobs that each member of your family performs on a regular basis to help the family live together, stay healthy, and survive. You may share these descriptions by telling them to another student working on this same assignment or by writing them on paper and reading them to another student. Draw pictures to show each family member doing his/her job.

Tier Two (middle readiness)

Students working at this tier complete the following tasks individually:

1) Interview a parent, grandparent, aunt, uncle, or any adult in your family who you know well. Your reason for interviewing this person is to find out how life for him/her was the same and how it was different when the person was your age. Use the questions on the worksheet that your teacher gives you. If you have a tape recorder, you may ask the adult if you can tape the interview. If you do not have a tape recorder, ask the adult to write his/her answers on the worksheet as the person talks with you.

2) Next, use the answers from your interview to create a short book to show how life in your family has changed from one generation to the next. One page will describe the adult you interviewed, and the page across from it will describe you. Put one fact on a page, and include a picture to illustrate what you said. You may write the facts yourself, use a computer to type and print the facts, or ask an adult to write what you dictate to them. Your teacher will help you bind the pages of your book. When it is finished, share the book with your class.

Suppose you are seven years old and you interviewed your mom. A page of your book might look like this:

When my mom was 7 years old...	Today, when I am 7 years old...
She read books during the week when she finished her homework.	I go to soccer practice and play games on my Xbox 360 when I finish my homework.

Tier Three (higher readiness)

Students assigned to this tier complete the following activities individually.

Your goal is to find out information about the history of your family.

1) You need the help of a family member for this first task. Ask your mom, dad, grandparents, or aunts and uncles to help you locate any of the following:
   - ✓ Old photographs of family members, especially ones showing something they were doing together.
   - ✓ Old letters written by family members that someone has saved.
   - ✓ Old documents, such as newspaper articles, certificates, or armed services records that relate to any information about family members.
   - ✓ Antiques or other items that are important to your family.

2) Ask your mom or dad which of your relatives knows the most about your family's history. Create five questions to ask this person. Write them or dictate them to an adult. The questions can be about any topic concerning your family. If you have a tape recorder, you may ask the adult if you can tape the interview. If you do not have a tape recorder, ask the adult to write his/her answers on a piece of paper as the person talks with you.

3) Use the information you gathered in the first two tasks to create a scrapbook about your family's history. Include some photographs of your choice, any documents or letters that you have found, and the information you got from your interview. Use tag board, poster board, or a picture album from a store to create your scrapbook. When it is completed, share your book with others working on this assignment so they can learn something about your family's history. Then take the scrapbook home and give it to your family as a gift.

Questions for Interviewing a Member of My Family

Think back to when you were the same age as I am. Answer these questions about life when you were that age.

1. How are we related?

2. Where were you living – the town, city, or country – when you were my age?

3. How did you get to school?

4. Were you on any sports team?

5. Did you take any kind of lessons, such as music lessons?

6. What was your favorite food?

7. Did you have homework? How much?

8. What was your favorite thing to do on a school afternoon when you had finished any homework?

9. How many brothers and sisters did you have?

10. Was there one activity that your family always did together? What was it?

11. Were you allowed to watch TV? If so, what was your favorite program?

12. Describe how you would spend a perfect Saturday afternoon.

Key American Historical Figures

Overview: *These tiered assignments require students to synthesize their under-standing of the contributions and impacts of the historical figures common to most state curricula while working at appropriate levels of challenge.* Assign tasks to the students based on their understandings of American history and the people who have im-pacted our society. Use these assignments in conjunction with more formal evaluations to assess students' knowledge and understanding of particular periods in U.S. history.

Standard:
  ➤ Identify and describe how key historical figures helped to shape the state and nation
Objectives:
The students will **KNOW**
  • The essential contributions and impacts of figures such as George Washington, Tho-mas Jefferson, Abraham Lincoln, Thurgood Marshall, Martin Luther King, Jr., Paul Revere, Clara Barton, Sojourner Truth, Frederick Douglass, and Harriet Tubman
The students will **UNDERSTAND THAT**
  • Some famous historical individuals were ordinary individuals who, due to unique cir-cumstances and personal conviction, rose to the occasion to become leaders.
  • People can contribute to and impact their societies in a variety of ways.
The students will **BE ABLE TO**
  • Describe key contributions of individuals from our nation's history.
  • Identify characteristics of good citizenship such as a belief in justice, truth, equality, and responsibility for the common good.
  • Work independently.
  • Use planning strategies to complete projects.
Materials:
  • Assorted art supplies

Closure: When the students have completed their assignments, allow time for them to share their products. Then, the class works together to create a time line that illustrates, in chronological order, the contributions made by the historical figures highlighted in the students' products. The class can also discuss which of the figures made the greatest contributions to America, supporting their opinions with factual information.

(Note: Add or substitute other important Americans as needed based on your course or state objectives.)

Tier One (lower readiness)

Students assigned to this tier work in pairs to complete the following task:

Create a scrapbook titled *"The Lives and Contributions of Some Great Americans."* Using both pictures (that you either draw or find on the Internet) and words, create multiple scrapbook pages about at least five of the following people: George Washington, Thomas Jefferson, Abraham Lincoln, Thurgood Marshall, Martin Luther King, Jr., Paul Revere, Clara Barton, Sojourner Truth, Frederick Douglass, and Harriet Tubman. Address the following types of information about each person (where applicable):

- ✓ Early years: birth place and date, childhood, education
- ✓ Family
- ✓ Work
- ✓ Challenges overcome
- ✓ Successes and major contributions to society and our country's history
- ✓ Interesting facts that most people may not know

Your scrapbook pages must be neat, legible, and well organized.

Tier Two (middle readiness)

Students working at this tier work in small groups of no more than four students to complete the following task:

You are a group of museum curators who have been chosen to create a comprehensive exhibit titled *"Important Americans."* You have been told that your exhibit must address at least five of the following people: George Washington, Thomas Jefferson, Abraham Lincoln, Thurgood Marshall, Martin Luther King, Jr., Paul Revere, Clara Barton, Sojourner Truth, Frederick Douglass, and Harriet Tubman. First, you must decide which five to include in your exhibit, and write a short explanation outlining and defending your choices. This statement will be the introduction to the exhibit. Then create, using both pictures and words, a detailed plan for your exhibit. What artifacts, illustrations, and written information will you include in your exhibit and why? How will you make your exhibit enticing and interesting to museum visitors?

Tier Three (higher readiness)

Students assigned to this tier work in pairs to complete the following task:

Create a panel discussion in which five of the following individuals talk to an audience of "history buffs" about their lives and contributions to America: George Washington, Thomas Jefferson, Abraham Lincoln, Thurgood Marshall, Martin Luther King, Jr., Paul Revere, Clara Barton, Sojourner Truth, Frederick Douglass, and Harriet Tubman. Through the use of interesting and engaging questions (that you must create!), have these people talk to the audience not only about themselves but also about what they think every American can and should do for his or her country. The panel members' responses must be based on historical fact and on the individuals' specific interests and contributions.

Map-Reading Skills

<u>**Overview**</u>: *These tiered activities provide practice with applying map-reading skills to solve a real-life problem.* Conduct an overview of map-reading essentials for the whole class prior to working on their assigned tasks. Then introduce students to the essential problem, as outlined below.

Standard:
➢ Explain geographic concepts and the relationship between people and geography in real-life situations

Objectives:

The students will **KNOW**
- Parts of a map.
- Symbols on a map.

The students will **UNDERSTAND THAT**
- Maps are useful instruments for helping people understand how to move around effectively.
- Maps contain coded information (e.g. compass rose, legends, keys, and scales) that is helpful to the map reader in selecting the most efficient routes.
- Selection of appropriate maps is essential to locating community resources.

The students will **BE ABLE TO**
- Use map terminology to describe and explain variations in the physical environment, such as the local community.
- Plan effective and efficient routes of movement using a given map.
- Gather information from a map in order to compare specific places or regions.

Materials:
- Several copies of a map of your local community. On this map, indicate the location of a fire and a fire house. After reading the assignment below, the teacher may decide to make the location of the fire be, perhaps, a public park or even a large store or warehouse. Either way, the teacher should take care in the selection of the fire's location.
- Overhead masters of the map
- Highlighters, pencils, and notebook paper

Closure: When they have finished, students share the nature of their roles and the associated tasks with the rest of the class.

(Note: The following activities assume that there are three different levels of readiness present in the class with regard to map-reading skills.)

✓ Tier One is for students who are still struggling with basic map-reading skills. Their task is simply to use a map and its features to go from point A to point B. It is assumed that, due to this group's lack of skills, the teacher will probably be working with these students to help them complete the exercise. Based on the students' needs, the teacher may decide to scale back some of the requirements or directions listed for these students.

✓ Students working on Tier Two already know how to read a map fairly well. These students are using their map skills to solve a particular problem and answer a certain set of questions.

✓ Tier Three is for students who are comfortable enough with map reading to tackle a more open-ended, "messier" application of that skill in real life. Afterwards, they must evaluate their actions to decide on the effectiveness of their choices.

Finally, the sophistication of the map provided to the students in some way affects the overall complexity and difficulty of the assignment. Use discretion and due judgment in selecting the type of map to be used for this exercise. Some classes of students might be just fine using a standard city map, while others may benefit from one designed and drawn by the teacher.

Introduction for All Students

A terrible threat faces your community! Earlier today, a horrible fire started somewhere in your city. Its flames grew and the fire spread in a very short period of time. Emergency crews were called out, and since this morning, they have continued to battle the fire bravely. You have a role in helping to keep your community safe!

Your teacher will give you a map that shows the location of this fire. He or she will also assign you and your group some very important roles which you must assume as you help to contain this fire. Take your job seriously! The future of your community is in your hands.

Tier One (lower readiness)

Your job is perhaps the most important. **You are to play the role of the 911 Dispatcher.**

You received a cell phone call from the first driver who happened by the scene of the fire. Because of this, you and your team were able to pinpoint the location of the fire. You immediately called the fire department who sent out a crew to investigate. Because they were unfamiliar with the location, you and your crew, using this map, charted the most direct way to lead the fire fighters to the scene.

Planning as a group, use the map to re-create the most direct route from the fire department to the scene of the fire. Then create a transcript of your conversation between the fire truck driver and yourself as he drove from the fire department to the location of the fire. You may either write this, or if you prefer, you may record it. Either way, be sure to use the map's compass rose, scale, and legend to give accurate directions.

To get you started your transcript might begin as follows:

"Make a _____ (left/right) turn out of the driveway of the firehouse onto _____ (name of the road) and proceed approximately ____ (number) miles _____ (direction) to the intersection with _____ (name of road)."

Be ready to share this with the rest of the class.

Tier Two (middle readiness)

You and your group members are the team meteorologists at the local news station. As the fire grows more and more intense, so too does the smoke. There is so much smoke that the fire department is worried about the worsening condition of the air quality and danger to nearby inhabitants. They are worried that a shift in the wind's direction could put locals in danger, as either the fire spreads or the smoke blows in their direction.

Your task is to analyze the location of the fire and, using the map, to answer the following questions:

- ✓ The fire department is worried that any neighborhood streets within a quarter-mile of the fire scene might be touched by the flames, while those located further out than that might only have to deal with the large volume of smoke. If the wind changes direction so that it blows from north to south, which streets will be affected by this? Are there any neighborhood streets in danger of catching on fire? If so, list them. Which will be affected by the smoke?

- ✓ Which direction would the wind have to blow in order for it to head towards your school? How many miles is the fire from your school?

- ✓ As you look at the map, are there any other communities or businesses near the site of the fire that may be affected by a change in wind direction? If so, list them, and give their direction and distance from the fire.

Be ready to share the results of your findings with the rest of the class.

Tier Three (higher readiness)

You and your team are members of the city's transportation department. Even as the fire is dying down, you and your team are rapidly planning routes to direct other drivers around the location of the danger. Because the wind has shifted direction, drivers are no longer being allowed to drive north towards the scene.

Using your map, you and your crew must create routes around the fire that will help drivers who wish to drive:

- ✓ from the north to the south
- ✓ from the east to the west
- ✓ from the west to the east

When you are done planning your routes, evaluate each one to decide on their effectiveness.

- ✓ Using an overhead that your teacher will give you, trace your routes.
- ✓ Make a pro and con list that summarizes the benefits and potential problems with your detours. For example, are there any places (hospitals or nursing homes, for example) or businesses that might be particularly affected by the sudden increase in traffic?

Be ready to discuss your task with the rest of the class.

Needs and Wants

Overview: *These tiered assignments ask students to apply their understandings of the differences between human needs and human wants while working at appropriate levels of challenge.* Introduce the differences between needs and wants with the class prior to assigning these tasks. Possibilities for this introduction include:

❖ Showing store-bought items such as foods and small toys and asking students to justify whether or not they are needs or wants.

❖ Writing short lists of needs and wants on the board or an overhead and asking students to identify which list includes things we need and which list includes things we might want. Students can be invited to add their own ideas to the lists.

Standard:
➢ Apply basic economic principles

Objectives:
The students will **KNOW**
- The definitions of *need* and *want*.

The students will **UNDERSTAND THAT**
- All living things have needs that must be met in order to survive.
- It is more important to have our needs met than to have things we want.
- It is sometimes difficult to distinguish between our needs and our wants, but it is important to be able to do so.
- We satisfy our needs and wants in many different ways.

The students will **BE ABLE TO**
- Identify examples of needs and wants.
- Distinguish between needs and wants.
- Evaluate needs and wants.
- Discuss how needs and wants are met.
- Make thoughtful and wise decisions.

Materials:
- Ox-Cart Man by Donald Hall
- Magazines, newspapers, store flyers, and catalogs
- Scissors, glue
- Several "yellow pages" phone books

Tier One (lower readiness)

Students working at this tier work as a group with the teacher to read the book Ox-Cart Man by Donald Hall. Once they have finished listening to the story, they create a list of the items in the story that meets the family's needs and another list showing the items that meet the family's wants. The teacher posts the lists so that all the students in the group can see them.

Once they have finished their group activity, the students work independently to write and illustrate lists of their own needs and wants. They may use their group lists based *on* Ox-Cart Man as support, but each student must create his or her own lists. When they have completed their lists, the students circle an item on their needs list that they think is the most important need they have. They do the same with an item on their wants list. They then share their lists with others working at this tier.

Once the students have finished their lists and have shared them with others, they come together as a group to discuss their needs and wants with the teacher. What are some things that they need? What are some things that they want? How can we tell the difference between a need and a want? Where might they go to find things that meet their needs? What about their wants?

Tier Two (middle readiness)

Students assigned to this tier work in pairs using pictures found in magazines, newspapers, store flyers, and catalogs to create collages showing needs and wants. They label their collages as needed to clarify the differences between needs and wants.

Once they have finished their collages, the students work independently to create short stories that include both needs and wants. Their stories may be about themselves or about others, but each story must include at least 5 needs and 5 wants and must explain how these needs and wants might be met. For example, if the story involves a child needing food, where might the child find food in his or her community?

Tier Three (higher readiness)

Students assigned to this tier work in groups of 3-4 students with the following prompt:

Imagine that you are given the opportunity to start your own small town. You don't have much time or money, but you know that it will be important to provide for the townspeople's needs and wants. Otherwise, they won't want to live in your town.

Create a list of the townspeople's needs. Create a second list showing their possible wants. Now, knowing that you can't provide everything, what are the things that are *most important* to provide for the townspeople, and how will you make sure they get them? To show your thinking, create a map of your town along with a yellow pages phone book so that the townspeople will know where to go when they need or want something. Look at the phone books provided so that you will know how to design one.

Closure: The students come together as a class to share and discuss their work and to respond to the following questions:
  • What are some examples of people's needs?
  • What are some examples of people's wants?
  • How do we get our needs met?
  • How do we get some things we want?
  • What would happen if your needs weren't met?
  • What would happen if you didn't get everything you wanted?
  • Is it more important for your needs or your wants to be met? Why?

Roles and Services in Communities

Overview: *The following assignments serve as culminating tasks for a study of the roles that people play and the services they provide in their communities.* Following discussions and activities designed to address various community members' roles, the teacher will assign the following tasks based on students' participation and work during the previous discussions and activities.

Standards:
- ➢ Analyze multiple roles in communities
- ➢ Elaborate on the value of community services

Objectives:

The students will **KNOW**
- • The titles of many different community members (for example, mayor, grocer, teacher).
- • The needs of community members.

The students will **UNDERSTAND THAT**
- • Communities are made up of a variety of different people who perform different roles and provide different services.
- • Community members need and want the services provided in their communities.
- • Communities are stronger when people work together to meet their needs and wants.

The students will **BE ABLE TO**
- • Describe the roles that people play in communities.
- • Compare, contrast, and evaluate community roles.

Materials:
- • Copies of *"Roles in a Community"* (for Tier One) provided in this lesson
- • Paper, markers, crayons, etc.

Closure: Pose the following questions to the whole group:
- • Which community role do you think is most important? Why?
- • Which roles do you think a community could do without? Why?
- • What would happen if we removed all sanitation workers from a community? What about leaders? (Ask several times using different community roles.)
- • Which roles would you like to have in a community? Why?

Tier One (lower readiness)

Students working at this tier complete the following tasks in pairs:

1) Brainstorm at least 10 different community roles. These may include roles that we have discussed as well as others that you know.

2) Complete the *"Roles in a Community"* table, showing detailed information about 6 of the roles you listed in step #1.

3) Draw a detailed picture that shows a variety of different community roles and the services that are provided by them.

Tier Two (middle readiness)

Students assigned to this tier work in pairs to complete the following tasks:

1) Brainstorm at least 12 different community roles. These may include roles that we have discussed as well as others that you know.

2) Sort the roles you brainstormed into 3 different groups, and label each group. What are the differences and similarities among the roles? How can they be grouped based on their differences and similarities? Have your teacher check your groups and labels.

(Note: For the next task, it helps if the students' groups are clearly defined. For example, their groups may address the roles of community leaders versus the roles of service providers such as doctors and postal workers.)

3) Select one role from each of your 3 groups. Create a conversation among these 3 roles in which each discusses the services he or she provides and his or her impact on the community. Each role must make a strong case for its importance.

Tier Three (higher readiness)

Students assigned to this tier complete the following in small groups of no more than 4 students:

1) Discuss what makes a person's role important in a community. How do you know when a role is one that a community cannot survive without?

2) On a large sheet of paper, draw the following continuum, leaving room to add terms:

Least important -- **Most important**

3) Place the following roles on the continuum, as well as 6 more of your choosing: mayor, teacher, sanitation worker, bus driver, judge, road crew worker, nurse, and animal control worker.

4) Write a paragraph that explains how your group decided where to place the roles on the continuum.

Roles in a Community

Community Role	What this person does, the services he or she provides	The tools and equipment this person uses	Importance to the community (1 is not at all important, 5 is very important)

Learning Profile-Based Language Arts

Little House on the Prairie

Overview: *These culminating project options allow students to demonstrate their understanding of the characters and events in* **Little House on the Prairie** *by Laura Ingalls Wilder.* As the reading of the novel comes to an end, share the project options with students so they can begin to select the options that most interest them. The students work independently on their chosen tasks, and they can evaluate their work using the project rubric provided. When the project options are discussed with the students, share the rubric so the students understand the expectations for their work.

Standards:
➢ Interact with texts before, during, and after reading, listening, or viewing
➢ Respond to texts using interpretive, critical, and evaluative processes

Objectives:
The students will **KNOW**
 • The characters and places in Little House on the Prairie.
 • Details highlighted in Little House on the Prairie.
The students will **UNDERSTAND THAT**
 • People are influenced by the times and places in which they live.
 • We can make meaningful connections to literature.
The students will **BE ABLE TO**
 • Recall details from the text.
 • Make connections to the text.
 • Draw conclusions, make generalizations, and gather support by referencing the text.
 • Compare and contrast.
 • Make decisions.
 • Work independently.

Materials:

- Multiple copies of Little House on the Prairie by Laura Ingalls Wilder
- Paper, pencils, markers, crayons, scissors, glue
- Copies of the Little House on the Prairie Final Project Rubric

Closure: Provide time for the students to share their products in small groups comprised of students who completed the same project options. For example, all students who worked on Option #1 meet together to share their work. In their small groups, the students evaluate one another's work and select one product from the group to share with the whole class. Thus, only one of each of the five possible products will be shared with all of the students.

Little House on the Prairie Final Project Options

Choose two (2) from the following options. Be sure to choose projects that allow you to show what you know and understand about the novel and that you enjoy completing. Your work must be:

✓ *Accurate*: It should show that you recall the people, events, and facts presented in the book.

✓ *Thoughtful*: It should be clear that you have put time into your work and that you have thought about the ideas you have included. When possible, your work should include connections to your own life, to the world around you, or to other stories.

✓ *Detailed*: Your work should include many specific facts about the story and/or about your life (depending on the projects you choose).

✓ *Original*: It should be your own work, and the ideas included should be yours.

✓ *Neat*: Your writing should be clear and legible, and any illustrations should be neat and clean. Your work should look like a final draft!

Option #1

_____ Imagine you can have lunch with a character/person from the book. Who would you choose? Why? Write a paragraph explaining your choice. What questions would you ask him or her? Why? After you list the questions, predict what answers the character might provide. (Minimum of 4 questions!)

Option #2

_____ Imagine that a character/person from the book could visit us in our time. What do you think he or she would like and dislike about the world now? Make a chart showing the likes and dislikes. What questions might he or she ask? How might you answer them? List both the questions and your answers. (Minimum of 4 questions!)

Option #3

_____ What is the same about the Ingalls girls' lives and your life? What is different? Find a way to tell others about the similarities and differences. Assuming you could take your family, friends, and pets with you, if you could live in their time and place, would you? Why or Why not? Write a paragraph explaining your answer.

Option #4

_____ You are Laura. Write a letter to your family and friends back in Wisconsin telling them all about your life on the prairie. Remember that this is the only letter you can send them for a long time. Give them lots of information and details! Make sure that your letter allows them to create a picture in their minds of your life on the prairie.

Option #5

_____ Imagine that a character from the book kept a scrapbook of the Ingalls' life on the prairie. What might be in the scrapbook? Create a copy of the scrapbook, and be sure to identify the character who originally made it. Design at least 5 pages in your scrapbook, including both words and pictures. Show the highs and lows of life on the prairie.

Little House on the Prairie Final Project Rubric

	Top Notch	Middle of the Road	Needs Help
Accuracy	I recalled correctly many details from the story and did not make up anything.	I recalled several details from the story correctly, but I wasn't sure on a few things so I just made them up.	I don't remember much from the story. I made up almost all of the information for my project.
Thoughtfulness	I put a lot of thought into my work and made several interesting and reasonable connections.	I put some thought into my work, but I got a little tired of all the thinking. I made some connections, but I am not sure they all make sense.	I tried not to work too hard on and think too much about my project.
Detail	I included many details and lots of description in my project. It is easy to "see" what I am describing in my writing.	I included some details, but my descriptions are not always as clear as they could be.	I did not include many details at all in my project.
Originality	My work and my ideas are mine, all mine.	Most of my ideas are my own, though I did borrow from others here and there.	Almost none of the ideas in my project are mine, and I "borrowed" many ideas from my classmates.
Neatness	None of my work is messy, and all of my writing is clear and easy to read.	Most of my work is neat, but I had to rush to finish some of my project. Some of it could be neater.	My project is a mess.

Elements of Poetry

Overview: *These culminating, learning profile-based activities provide students with opportunities to creatively explore some of the key terminology associated with a standard, elementary unit on poetry.* Students choose the tasks they want to complete. The number of tasks that each student completes and whether students can work with others on their tasks is left to the discretion of the teacher.

Standards:
> ➤ Compose a variety of written selections using self-selected and assigned topics and forms (e.g., poems, simple narratives, short reports, learning logs, letters, notes, directions, and instructions)
> ➤ Read a variety of texts, including poetry

Objectives:
The students will **KNOW**
- Vocabulary including *tone, imagery, figurative language, simile, metaphor,* and *hyperbole.*

The students will **UNDERSTAND THAT**
- An author uses figurative language to create a tone and to help create an image in the mind of the reader.
- Figurative language includes expressions of written imagery such as similes, metaphors, hyperbole, and others.
- Poetry, like other written expressions of creativity, may follow certain conventions.
- The language and visuals of poetic expression bring characters or topics to life, enhance narrative development, and produce a response in the reader.

The students will **BE ABLE TO**
- Write effective narratives, poems, and explanations.
- Write rhymed, unrhymed, and patterned poetry.
- Describe the characteristics of free verse, rhyme, and patterned poetry (including haiku, narrative, concrete, etc.).
- Respond to written assignments using interpretive, critical, and evaluative processes by participating in creative interpretations.

Materials:
- Copies of the attached RAFT assignment

Closure: Once the students' RAFT assignments are completed, review some of the essentials of the poetry unit by asking students to share their work.

Elements of Poetry

ROLE	AUDIENCE	FORMAT	TOPIC
The word "orange" (or "purple")	Advice columnist	A "Dear Abby" letter	I'm sad because I have no **rhyming word** buddies like "blue" and "pink" do.
A flower	A bee	A set of **haikus**	I love your company.
Advertiser	Magazine reader	**Concrete poem**	Check this product out! (Your written ad should be in the shape of your chosen product.)
A child	A parent	A Mother/Father's Day card of illustrated **similes**	All the ways you are so important to me.
General manager at a radio station	Potential radio DJ sitting for an interview	A written list of **alliterative** tongue twisters	"To show me you would be a good DJ, you've got to say..."
Museum interpreter for the blind	A blind person	A descriptive speech (full of **imagery** that appeals to all the senses)	"Before you is..." (Select a picture or a sculpture to describe with rich details)
A student	Your teacher	**Narrative poem**	The first day of school
Starving artist	Author of a children's book of riddles (**puns**)	Illustrations	"I think these pictures would illustrate your jokes very well."
Rhyming, metered poem	**Free verse** poem	Personal letter	"You are so lucky... You don't have to follow as many rules as I do."
Author of a book about an American tall tale character (you choose the character)	Book editor	A page of exaggerated descriptions about the character...examples of **hyperbole**. ("Paul Bunyan was taller than a skyscraper.")	"Here are my revisions to make the story more exciting."
David Letterman	Late night talk show audience	Top 10 list	Cheesiest **metaphors** that describe love ("Your love is the butter on my toast.")
Sports team advertiser (you choose the sport and the team)	Car driver	A **rhyming couplet** bumper sticker	We have the best team!

James and the Giant Peach

Overview: *These RAFT assignments give students the opportunity to work in ways that mirror their learning profiles while synthesizing their understanding of the novel* **James and the Giant Peach** *by Roald Dahl.* Each student completes one task from the options presented, and the students' work can be used in combination with a more formal assessment as the cumulative assessment for this novel study.

Standards:
➤ Apply strategies and skills to comprehend text that is read, heard, and viewed
➤ Respond to various texts

Objectives:
The students will **KNOW**
• The plot, characters, and settings of James and the Giant Peach.
• The characteristics of the plot, characters, and settings in James and the Giant Peach.

The students will **UNDERSTAND THAT**
• Characters in stories have particular personalities.
• The setting of a story is important to what happens in the story.
• Stories have beginnings, middles, and ends.

The students will **BE ABLE TO**
▪ Recall facts and details from a story.
• Describe characters, settings, and plots.
• Work independently.
• Use planning strategies to complete projects.

Materials:
• Multiple copies of James and the Giant Peach by Roald Dahl
• Copies of the attached RAFT assignment
• Magazines
• Scissors, glue, markers, crayons, etc.

Closure: Rather than giving each student time to share his or her product with the whole class, create mixed-learning profile groups (include each of the different RAFT options in a group), and allow time for the students to share their work in these smaller groups. Once all the students have had time to share their products, ask them discuss as a whole group their favorite characters in and parts of James and the Giant Peach.

James and the Giant Peach

ROLE	AUDIENCE	FORMAT	TOPIC
Newspaper reporter	Newspaper readers	Written interview with a character in the story (include at least 5 questions and the character's answers to them)	What should we learn from this story and why?
Panel moderator and 5 characters in the story	TV audience	Panel discussion with at least 5 characters (include questions and answers)	Why everyone should read this book
Yourself	Your classmates	Riddles (at least 10, written or audiotape)	Can you guess these events, characters, and places from James and the Giant Peach?
Visual artist	Literary museum curator	Visual time line (either illustrated by hand or shown with pictures from magazines) with its corresponding museum plaque ex-plaining your choices	The Top 10 Events in James and the Giant Peach and why I chose them
Roald Dahl	Elementary students	Speech including details from the novel	What I'd like my book to teach you about friendship

Exploring Character, Setting, and Plot in Literature

Overview: *These tiered Think-Tac-Toes give students the opportunity to work independently and at appropriate levels of challenge while describing and analyzing the characters, settings, and plot of a particular story.* Because they are generic in nature, use these Think-Tac-Toes with almost any story and modify as needed to better fit a particular story.

For each tier, the rows focus on different literary elements (these are the same for both tiers): character, setting, or plot. Assign students to a particular tier and then have them choose one task from each row on their Think-Tac-Toe to complete a total of three tasks. While they can work on their tasks in any order they choose, each student will ultimately be working with all three literary elements included on the Think-Tac-Toes. This approach not only provides students with choice based on their learning profiles, but it also ensures that they address each of the highlighted literary elements. It is best to assign these tasks once students have had a chance to listen to and/or read and to discuss a particular story.

Standards:
- ➤ Apply strategies and skills to comprehend text that is read, heard, and viewed
- ➤ Respond to various texts
- ➤ Analyze the characteristics of texts

Objectives:

The students will **KNOW**
- • The story elements (character, setting, and plot) of a particular story.
- • The characteristics of different characters, settings, and plots.

The students will **UNDERSTAND THAT**
- • Characters in stories have particular personalities.
- • We can describe characters based on their words and actions.
- • The setting of a story is important to what happens in the story.
- • Stories have beginnings, middles, and ends.

The students will **BE ABLE TO**
- Recall facts and details from a story.
- Describe characters, settings, and plots.
- Compare and contrast.
- Justify thinking and defend choices.
- Work independently.
- Use planning strategies to complete projects.

Materials:
- Multiple copies of a particular story
- Paper, pencils, crayons, markers, scissors, glue
- Magazines
- Copies of the Think-Tac-Toe

Closure: Allow time for the students to share their products in small, mixed-readiness groups.

Exploring Character, Setting, and Plot in Literature
(Tier One)

1) Describe your favorite character using as many words as you can. You may also use pictures.	2) Write (or dictate) a diary entry that your favorite character might write. What would he or she say about a day in his or her life?	3) Use a Venn diagram (double-bubble map) to compare yourself and your favorite character. What do you have in common? How are you different?
4) Draw a map of the setting of the story. What places are most important in the story? Where are they? Be sure to label your map!	5) Make a collage that shows the different settings in the story. Label your collage so that we can understand how the pictures you chose relate to the settings in the story.	6) Using words and pictures, compare the main setting of the story to the place where you live. How are they alike? How are they different?
7) Illustrate 3 events in the story on 3 separate pieces of paper. Use words to help us better understand your illustrations. Then put your illustrations in the correct order.	8) Draw and write about an important part of the story. Why did you pick this part? Be ready to explain your choice.	9) Compose a new title for the story that tells something about what happens in the story. Why did you choose this title? Be ready to explain your choice.

Exploring Character, Setting, and Plot in Literature
(Tier Two)

1) Describe your favorite character from the point of view of another character. What might he or she really think about your favorite character?	2) Write (or dictate) a diary entry that your favorite character might write on a good day and one that he or she might write on a bad day. How would these diary entries be different?	3) Find a way to compare your favorite character to a character in another story. What do the characters have in common? How are they different?
4) Draw a map of the most important place in the story. Why is this place important to the characters in the story? Be sure to label your map!	5) Make a time line that shows how and when the setting of the story changes. Label your time line so that we will understand your ideas.	6) What if the story took place in another location? Change the setting of the story. How will this change the story? What might happen now?
7) Make a time line of the events in the story. You should have no more than 8 events on your time line. How will you choose what to include?	8) Make a list of the most important events in the story. Then make a second list of the least important events in the story. How did you decide where to place these events? Be ready to explain your thinking.	9) Change one part of the story. How does this change the whole story? How will the story end now? Why?

Learning Profile-Based Math

Telling Time

Overview: *Students select an activity from the following options, all of which ask them to work with telling time.* The options are based on Gardner's Theory of Multiple Intelligences. Before completing these tasks, give students ample practice with telling time.

Standard:
  ➢ Read time using analog clocks

Objectives:
The students will **KNOW**
  • The parts of an analog clock (face, hands, numbers representing hours and minutes).
The students will **UNDERSTAND THAT**
  • Telling time is an important skill that people use all the time.
The students will **BE ABLE TO**
  • Read times on an analog clock.
  • Show times on an analog clock.
  • Explain how to tell time on an analog clock.

Materials:
  • Paper, pencils, crayons, markers
  • Index cards or small pieces of paper
  • String or yarn
  • Small, manipulative clocks for student use
  • Small chalkboards or whiteboards
  • Chalk or whiteboard markers

Closure: Once students have completed their chosen tasks, the teacher should pose the following questions to the whole group:
  • What makes telling time difficult?
  • What do you think is the most important thing to know about telling time?
  • Why is being able to tell time an important skill? How do people use this skill?
  • What might happen if you can't tell time?

Telling Time Task Options

Option #1

_____ Imagine that you meet someone who does not know how to tell time. How will you help that person learn to tell time? Work with a partner to create a set of directions to help others learn this important skill. What is the first step in telling time? What is the second step? How many steps are there in all? Make your directions very clear and detailed so that someone can really use them. Include a detailed illustration of a clock and its parts to add to your set of directions.

Option #2

_____ *(Students will need assistance from the teacher with this particular option)* Work with 2-3 other students to create a clock face on the floor of the classroom. Where will the numbers go? How will you show them? Now, what can you use for the hands on the clock? Once you have created the face and hands, practice showing different times on your big clock. One student can call out times while the other students show it on the group's clock.

Option #3

_____ Create a six-panel cartoon that shows illustrations of activities that might occur at specific times during the day. Each of the six panels must include an analog clock that shows the time of the activity as well as a picture of the activity. You may include dialogue in your panels as well.

Option #4

_____ Take turns with a partner showing and telling times on analog clocks. Write on a small chalkboard or whiteboard the times that you and your partner practice showing and telling. Once you have each had at least 6 turns showing and telling times, look at the times you practiced. You should have at least 12 times in all. Now, add 5 minutes to each time. What times will you have now? Show those times on your clocks.

Fractions

Overview: *These RAFT assignments give students opportunities to apply their knowledge of fractional amounts in ways that address their learning-profile strengths.* Have students make a choice, or choices, from the options presented and complete the work independently. The teacher can decide how many options the students complete.

Standards:
  ➢ Divide regions and sets to represent a fraction
  ➢ Represent fractions concretely and symbolically
  ➢ Compare and order fractions using models and benchmark numbers
  ➢ Compare fractions to show equivalency

Objectives:

The students will **KNOW**
  • A *fraction* is a way of representing part of a whole or part of a group; fractions are used to name a part of one thing or a part of a collection of things.
  • The language of fractions.
  • *Equivalent fractions* name the same amount.

The students will **UNDERSTAND THAT**
  • The denominator tells the number of equal parts in a whole and the numerator tells how many equal-sized parts are being considered.
  • In each fraction model, the parts must be equal (i.e., each pie piece must have the same area.)
  • Wholes are broken into equal-sized parts and reassembled into wholes.

The students will **BE ABLE TO**
  • Identify the numerator and denominator of a fraction and what they tell about the fractional amount.
  • Represent and name fractions concretely and symbolically.
  • Compare and order fractions from 1/2 to 1/12.
  • Differentiate between equivalent and non-equivalent fractions.

Materials:
- Copies of the RAFT choices
- Art materials for some choices
- Straight edge
- Pattern blocks

Closure: Rather than having each student share his or her product with the whole class, create mixed-learning profile groups including as many of the RAFT options as possible, and allow time for the students to share their work in these smaller groups. Display visual products in the room for all students to examine.

Fractions

ROLE	AUDIENCE	FORMAT	TOPIC
A large pizza (you get to pick the toppings)	Person who bought the pizza	Drawings of the pizza	Five different ways you can cut me into pieces (the pieces must be the same size on each individual pizza)
Numerator	Denominator	A friendly email	It's a good thing we are best friends because it takes both of us to name a fraction
A non-equivalent fraction	An equivalent fraction	An unfriendly email	What makes you think you are so special?
The fraction 1/4	The fraction 1/12	Storyboard	Why I'm a larger amount than you are
The fraction 1/3	An advice columnist (like Dear Abby)	Letter asking for help	Why can't I ever be a part of the whole number family?
Student	Teacher	Pattern blocks	Look at all the ways I can represent fractions using this set of blocks!
The fraction 1/2	People watching the Dave Letterman TV show	Top Ten List	The top ten equivalent fractions that name my same amount
Fractions	Math students	Brochure	Ways your lives would be different if we didn't exist

Points, Lines, Line Segments, Rays, and Angles

Overview: *These RAFT assignments give students opportunities to apply their knowledge of plane geometric figures in ways that address their learning-profile strengths.* Have students choose from the options presented and complete their work independently.

Standards:
> ➤ Identify, describe, and classify the properties of plane geometric figures
> ➤ Investigate and describe the relationships between and among points, lines, line segments, rays, and angles
> ➤ Identify lines that are parallel, intersecting, and perpendicular
> ➤ Distinguish between acute, obtuse, and right angles

Objectives:

The students will **KNOW**

- A *point* is an exact location in space with no length or width.
- A *line* is a collection of points going infinitely in both directions with no endpoints.
- *Intersecting lines* are lines that cross and have one point in common.
- *Perpendicular lines* are special intersecting lines that form right angles where they intersect.
- *Parallel lines* are lines that lie on the same flat surface and never cross, are always the same distance apart, and do not share any points.
- A *line segment* is part of a line that is determined by two endpoints and all the points between.
- A *ray* is part of a line that has one endpoint and continues to infinity in one direction.
- Two rays that have the same endpoint form an *angle*.
- A *right angle* is an angle that forms a square corner.
- An *acute angle* forms an angle less than a right angle.
- An *obtuse angle* forms an angle greater than a right angle.

The students will **UNDERSTAND THAT**

- Points, lines, line segments, rays, and angles are fundamental components of noncircular geometric figures.
- Relationships exist between points, lines, line segments, rays, and angles.
- Lines in a plane either intersect or are parallel, with perpendicularity being a special case of intersection.

The students will **BE ABLE TO**
- Differentiate between points, lines, line segments, rays, and angles.
- Identify lines that are parallel, intersecting, or perpendicular, using their definitions.
- Differentiate between right, acute, and obtuse angles.

Materials:
- Copies of the RAFT choices
- Art materials for some choices
- Straight edge

Closure: Rather than having each student share his or her product with the whole class, create mixed-learning profile groups including as many of the RAFT options as possible. Allow time for the students to share their work in these smaller groups.

Points, Lines, Line Segments, Rays, and Angles

ROLE	AUDIENCE	FORMAT	TOPIC
Cartoonist	Math students	Comic Strip	Ronnie Ray Meets Ann the Angle – Love at First Sight
One of two parallel lines	The second of two parallel lines	Poem	How Sad It Is that We Will Never Meet
A geometric plane	Points, lines, line segments, rays, and angles	A visual dictionary	How I Can Identify One of You from Another
Perpendicular lines	Right angles	Greeting card	Best Friends Forever
Right angle, acute angle, and obtuse angle	Math teachers	Persuasive letter	We Are All Equally Important to Your Geometry Lessons
Line	Line segment	Song	Without Me, You Would Be Nothing!
Point	Line, line segment, ray, and angle	Angry email	I'm Tired of Always Being Known as the Little Guy
Reporter	Readers of the newspaper	News story	End Points Are Missing – Line Segments, Rays, and Angles Fear for Their Lives!

Probability and Statistics

Overview: *These Think-Tac-Toe options allow students to choose their own ways of showing what they have come to know and understand about probability and its applications in the real world.* The tasks address student interest and personal choice. Students may choose any three options within the grid. Use this Think-Tac-Toe as one of the culminating activities for a unit on probability, and combine it with other formal assessments to evaluate student learning.

Standards:
- Collect, organize, and display data in a variety of ways (line graphs, bar graphs, circle graphs, line plots, etc.) to draw conclusions and make predictions
- Describe the distribution of a set of data using mean, median, mode, and range
- Record the possible outcomes of a simple event and systematically keep track of these outcomes when the event is repeated many times
- Conduct simple probability experiments
- Use the results of probability experiments to predict future events

Objectives:
The students will **KNOW**
- *Probability* is the chance of an event occurring.
- Probability can be expressed as a common fraction or a decimal.
- The purpose of a graph is to represent data gathered to answer a question.
- For any event, such as flipping a coin, the equally likely things that can happen are called *outcomes*.
- The *mean* of a number set is the sum of the numbers, divided by the total number of numbers in the set.
- The *median* of a number set is the middle value of the set.
- The procedure for determining the median differs depending on whether there is an odd or even number of numbers in the set.
- The *mode* of a number set is the most frequent value found in the set, the number that appears most often.
- A set can have more than one mode or no mode at all.
- The *range* of a set of numbers is the largest value in the set minus the smallest value in the set.

The students will **UNDERSTAND THAT**
- The actual probability of an event does not always equal the theoretical probability of an event.
- Data can be used to estimate the probability of future events.
- The larger the number of samples in a simulated experiment, the more likely the chance that the result approximates the theoretical probability.
- Data must be organized by listing values from smallest to largest in order to determine the mean, median, mode, and range.

The students will **BE ABLE TO**
- Conduct a probability experiment.
- Use the results of a probability experiment to predict the probability of future events.
- Organize data to calculate the mean, median, mode, and range.
- Use a variety of graphical methods to display, organize, and interpret data.

Materials (depending upon the activities chosen by the students):
- Copies of the Think-Tac-Toe
- A novel of choice
- 10 pictures/photographs of crowds of people
- A coin
- Dice
- A deck of playing cards
- A thermometer or access to the outside temperature.

Closure: The students share their data and predictions with one another in small groups. These groups may be randomly assigned or may consist of students who completed the same tasks. Encourage the students to discuss how accurate their predictions were and what they have learned about probability.

Probability and Statistics

Select a novel of your choice, and turn to a random page. Tally the number of times each of the five vowels in the alphabet appears on the page. Record your data on a line plot. Add the totals for each vowel. Report to the class the vowel that appeared most often and the one that appeared least often. If you were a player on "Wheel of Fortune," what advice does this survey give you?	Examine the ten pictures of crowds provided by your teacher. In each picture, count the number of people who are wearing glasses. Organize this data by listing the numbers from smallest to largest. Calculate the range, mean, median, and mode for the data collected.	Conduct a survey of the students in your classroom to record their eye color: brown, blue, hazel, green, or gray. Design a chart to collect and record the data. Then express as a fraction the probability of each eye color occurring. Based on this data, predict the number of students with each eye color in other classes your size. Collect data from several other classes in your school and compare the results to your predictions.
Conduct a survey of the students in your classroom to record the number of letters in their first and last names. Organize the data by listing the numbers from smallest to largest. Calculate the range, mean, median, and mode for the data collected.	Theoretically, tossing a coin gives you a 1/2 chance of tossing a head or a tail. Test this probability. Toss a coin 100 times, and record whether you tossed a head or a tail. Determine the probability of your experiment. How close were you to the theoretical probability?	Roll two dice 100 times and record how many times you roll each number, 2-12. Express the probability of rolling each of the numbers as fractions. Which number occurred most often? Which occurred least often? How would you predict board game makers would use this information when designing the game rules?
For one week (seven days), record the temperature at the exact same time each day. You may choose the time. Record your data on a line graph, with the day on one axis and the temperature on the other. Use your data to predict what the temperature will be for that time on the day <u>after</u> you stop your recording.	Using a deck of playing cards, conduct an experiment to determine the probability of drawing a face card (Jack, Queen, or King) from the deck. Shuffle the cards 50 different times, and have a partner or yourself draw one card after each shuffle. Record the number of times a face card is drawn, and calculate your probability of drawing a face card.	Conduct a survey of the students in your class to record their favorite after school activity. The six choices given are: visiting/playing with friends, playing sports, using computers, watching TV, reading a book, or communicating with friends using a phone, email, etc. Before collecting the data, predict which activity you believe will receive the most votes. After you finish the survey, record the data on a chart, and construct a bar graph to display the results. How close was your prediction?

Learning Profile-Based Science

Deserts

Overview: *These projects allow students to work either independently or with others to synthesize what they know and understand about deserts while working in ways that honor their different learning profiles.* The project options are based on Gardner's Theory of Multiple Intelligences and, thus, each student chooses one project that matches his or her intelligence preference. Students may also choose to work alone or with others (in groups of no more than four). Because these projects ask students to apply their understanding of deserts and can be used as an evaluation of their understanding, complete the following types of activities with the class to build knowledge and understanding prior to presenting the project options:

❖ Examine pictures of deserts and discuss their characteristics, including animal and plant life.
❖ Generate a class list of questions about deserts to be answered through readings and activities.
❖ Read and discuss a variety of books about deserts (for example, <u>Welcome to the Sea of Sand</u> by Jane Yolen and <u>The Desert is Theirs</u> by Byrd Baylor).
❖ Explore world maps and locate large deserts.
❖ Conduct a simple experiment to determine the water content of certain foods (place foods in baggies in a sunny spot or under a lamp and observe the condensation in the baggies).

Standard:
➢ Know that the world has different ecosystems that support different types of organisms
Objectives:
The students will **KNOW**
• The definition of a *desert*.
• Animals and plants that live in and can survive in deserts.
• The locations of different deserts around the world.

The students will **UNDERSTAND THAT**

- Deserts have characteristics that distinguish them from other ecosystems.
- A desert is defined by amount of rainfall, not temperature.
- Some animals and plants are designed to survive in deserts, but many animals and plants could not survive in deserts.

The students will **BE ABLE TO**

- Describe deserts.
- Identify desert animals and plants.
- Explain how different organisms (animals, plants, and humans) are able to survive in a desert.
- Make decisions and justify them.

Materials:

- Examples of catalogs

Closure: Allow time for the students to share their products in small, mixed-learning profile groups.

Desert Project Options

(Note: When introducing these projects, explain to students that their work must include information about the characteristics of deserts as well as the animal and plant life that inhabit them. Addressing only desert characteristics is not sufficient.)

The Storyteller

Imagine that you have trekked across a desert and have lived to tell about it. Write an adventure story that describes your travels. What did you encounter along the way? What dangers did you face? How did you survive and stay safe during your time in the desert? Be sure to include many details about your encounters, problems, and survival strategies. Someone else may benefit from your wisdom some day!

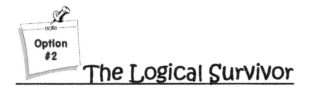

The Logical Survivor

You and a friend are preparing for a trek across a large desert. Your trip should last at least one week, assuming everything goes as planned. What will you take with you if you are certain to spend at least a week in the desert and not come across civilization during that time? Keep in mind that you will encounter animals, plants, and people along the way. Brainstorm the possible items.

Now, assume that you have a limited capacity for carrying items. You will have one camel (or another similar animal), but how much can one camel carry? Prioritize your items. What is the most important thing to take with you and why? What can you stand to leave behind? Create a rank-ordered list of items with a written explanation of their importance.

The Salesperson

You are the owner of an outdoor adventure supply company. Adventurers from all over the world shop your catalog for items they need. While you can't stock everything they might need, you do try to provide items that will sell and be of the best help to your customers. Many of your customers like to try "desert adventuring" so a section of your catalog focuses on that particular ecosystem. However, that particular section has grown outdated and needs revising.

Create the new desert section for your company's catalog. What items should be included? How much will they cost? How will you convince your customers to buy them? How can you make your catalog visually appealing and interesting? Keep in mind that you want to make some money, help your customers, and offer a wide range of items for a variety of survival needs!

The Solar System

Overview: *These RAFT assignments give students the opportunity to work in ways that mirror their learning profiles while synthesizing their understanding of a wide variety of learning objectives related to the solar system.* The teacher determines how many projects the students complete and at what points during a unit on the solar system.

Standard:
> Investigate and understand basic patterns and cycles occurring in nature, including the patterns of natural events such as day and night, seasonal changes, phases of the moon and tides, and movement of the planets in the solar system

Objectives:

The students will **KNOW**
- The seasons and what causes them.
- The cycles of phases of the moon and of tides and their causes.
- The relative size, position, age, and makeup of the Earth, moon, sun, and planets and how they compare to one another.

The students will **UNDERSTAND THAT**
- Relationships that exist between and among the Earth, sun, and moon result in day and night, seasonal changes, phases of the moon, and the tides.
- Due to its axial tilt, the Earth experiences seasons during its revolution around the sun.
- The pattern of seasonal changes takes place because the Earth's axis is tilted toward or away from the sun during its revolution around the sun.
- The pattern of day and night is caused by the one complete rotation of the Earth every 24 hours. The part of the Earth toward the sun has daylight while the part of the Earth away from the sun has night.
- The Earth is the third of eight planets that revolve around the sun and comprise the solar system.
- The phases of the moon follow a pattern.
- The tides follow a pattern of two high and two low tides every 24 hours. This pattern is caused for the most part by the gravitational attraction between the Earth and the moon.

The students will **BE ABLE TO**
- Explain how the Earth's rotation causes day and night.
- Explain how the sun's rays strike the Earth to cause seasons.
- Explain the phases of the moon.
- Explain high tide and low tide in relation to the moon.
- Describe the sun's general importance to life on Earth and its larger role as the center of our galaxy.

Materials:
- Copies of the attached RAFT assignment
- Scissors, paper, glue, markers, crayons, etc.

Closure: Create mixed-learning profile groups, including a variety of different RAFT options in each, and allow time for the students to share their work in these smaller groups.

The Solar System

ROLE	AUDIENCE	FORMAT	TOPIC
Revolution	Rotation	Letter of complaint (with diagram)	I hate it when people get us confused!
World's Scientists	Pluto's lawyer	Written response to the lawyer's Filing of Grievances ("You threw Pluto out of the Planet Club. Explain yourselves!")	Here's why Pluto was removed from the Planet Club.
U. S. travel agent	A client who wants to go to a warmer place during the winter	Recorded conversation between the agent and the client	Why it's summer in Australia when it's winter in the U.S.
Sunscreen lotion manufacturer	People going on vacation near the Equator	Television or newspaper advertisement	Why you'll REALLY need our product there!
Sun	Itself (the Sun)	Private diary/journal entry	Some humans are so confused about what "happens" to me at night....
Moon	A person who lived in the Dark Ages (before science was created)	A multi-panel cartoon .	I know you're confused. I get small, then big, then small, then big....Here's what's going on.
Ocean	Children who build sand castles	Lyrics to a song called "Blame It on the Moon"	It's not my fault that, twice a day, I leave and then come back to destroy sand castles.
Society of All Living Things on Earth	Sun	Award plaque: Most Important Source of Energy in the World	Why you deserve this award.
Mercury	Neptune	Letter	How our lives are different. (You may explain the differences in everything from how long a planetary year lasts to temperature of your surface to how fast you rotate on your axis.)

Weather

Overview: *These learning profile-based RAFT assignments give students an opportunity to apply their knowledge of weather conditions and phenomena that occur across the planet and to examine how these conditions and phenomena can be measured and predicted.* Students may complete their chosen tasks either individually or with partners, and it is left to the teacher to decide how many tasks each student must complete over the course of a unit on weather.

Standards:
- ➢ Investigate and understand basic types of, changes in, and patterns related to weather
- ➢ Investigate and determine how temperature, wind direction and speed, precipitation, cloud cover, and air pressure are affected by predictable patterns of weather
- ➢ Identify and explain the use of weather measurements and meteorological tools
- ➢ Describe and analyze the formation of various types of clouds and their relationship to weather fronts and storms

Objectives:

The students will **KNOW**
- The Earth's weather changes continuously from day to day.
- Extreme atmospheric conditions create various kinds of storms.
- Cloud formations are varied and can be used to predict short term weather conditions.

The students will **UNDERSTAND THAT**
- Changes in the weather are characterized by daily differences in wind, temperature, and precipitation.
- Weather data is collected and recorded using instruments that provide information useful for predicting weather and determining weather patterns.
- Meteorologists use data to predict weather patterns.
- Weather influences human activity.
- Extremes in the weather, such as too little or too much precipitation, can result in droughts or floods.

The students will **BE ABLE TO**
- Measure and record weather data using a variety of weather instruments, including (dependent upon grade level) a thermometer, rain gauge, weather vane, barometer, and anemometer.

- Differentiate between cloud types and the weather associated with each.
- Recognize a variety of storm types, describe the weather conditions associated with each, and explain when they occur.
- Compare and contrast droughts and floods.
- Identify common types of storms.

Materials:
- Reference materials about weather and storms
- Internet access for research and to download pictures
- Art materials to create picture books, including textured materials such as cotton or cloth
- Magazines with weather-related images and/or weather visuals downloaded from the Internet

---

Closure: Create mixed-learning profile groups, including a variety of different RAFT options in each group, and allow time for the students to share their work in these smaller groups.

Weather

ROLE	AUDIENCE	FORMAT	TOPIC
Mother Nature	All types of weather	Song or rap	Love Us or Hate Us, You Can't Live without Us
Temperature	Thermometer	Friendly email	Ways We Influence the Human Population Every Day
Hurricane	Tornado	Debate	I'm More Powerful Than You Are!
Severe Drought	Farmers	Letter of apology	Reasons Why You Are Not Getting Any Rain
David Letterman	Late Night TV Audience	Top Ten List	The Most Destructive Storms on Earth in the Last 100 Years
Artist	Visitors to an Art Gallery	Collage	Weather, Weather Everywhere!
Weather Instruments	Meteorologist	Conversation	Without Us, You Wouldn't Have a Job
Clouds	Earth's Human Population	A Picture Book	How to Visually Identify Our Types and Predict the Weather Conditions that Follow Us

Matter

<u>Overview</u>: *These Think-Tac-Toe options allow students to explore different aspects of matter. Specifically, students investigate matter's composition, what happens when one kind of matter interacts with another kind of matter (creating mixtures, solutions, compounds), and what happens as matter is heated or cooled.* By selecting one activity from each row of the Think-Tac-Toe, students address each of these objectives, while having choice in the final products generated. Use this Think-Tac-Toe with a whole class, giving all students a chance to explore the concepts of matter, or use it with students who might need enrichment during a unit addressing this topic.

The first row deals with the behavior of states of matter.

The second row deals with the differences between mixtures, solutions, and compounds.

Standard:
  ➢ Investigate and understand that *matter* is anything that has mass and takes up space
Objectives:
The students will **KNOW**
  • The states of matter (solid, liquid, gas).
  • Processes that cause changes in matter.
  • Vocabulary: *atoms, molecules, mixture, solution, compound, element, compound.*
The students will **UNDERSTAND THAT**
  • All matter, regardless of its size, shape, or color, is made of particles (atoms and molecules) that are too small to be seen by the unaided eye.
  • As temperature increases, most kinds of matter change from a solid to a liquid to a gas.
  • As temperature decreases, matter changes from a gas to a liquid to a solid.
  • There are many different types of compounds because atoms of elements combine in many different ways (and in different whole number ratios) to form different compounds.

The students will **BE ABLE TO**
- Describe the processes that cause matter to move from one state to another.
- Describe the interaction of the atoms or molecules as matter experiences a change in state.
- Compare and contrast mixtures and solutions, elements and compounds, and atoms and molecules.
- Construct and interpret a sequence of models (diagrams) showing the activity of molecules in all three states of matter.

Materials:
- Paper, pencils, crayons, markers, scissors
- A collection of magazines

Closure: When they have completed their chosen assignments, students share them in small groups. As a whole group, the teacher asks students to summarize the key ideas of the unit.

Matter

Search through a collection of magazines, and find as many examples as you can of solids, liquids, and gases. Cut them out, and make a collage of each state of matter using paper and glue. Since gases will be hard to find, you might have to find examples of objects that are associated with gas. For example, balloons, the steam rising from a cup of coffee, neon lights, etc. Create a fourth collage that shows changes in matter. How can you use pictures to show how matter behaves?	Imagine you are an ice cube sitting in a glass of iced tea outside on a sunny day. The owner of the glass has left you there to melt as he goes back to work in his yard. Write a journal entry from the ice's point view describing what it is like to: (1) melt from a solid piece of ice to a liquid, (2) merge with the tea, and then (3) evaporate from the glass into the air outside. Be sure to use lots of descriptive words and images. You may add pictures.	As matter changes from one state to another (for example, from a liquid to a gas), the movement of the molecules/atoms in that matter changes also. With others, create a demonstration, using both body movement and props, that shows what the molecules/atoms act like in each of the three states. Be sure to consider how packed together they are and how much movement they exhibit as they go from one state to another.
A *solution* is a mixture in which one substance dissolves in another. A common example would be that packet of Kool-Aid® you love so much. When you pour the powder into a pitcher of water and then stir it, you have created a tasty solution. Brainstorm a list of other common solutions and then categorize them. Are they cleaners? Drinks? Medicines? Others? Find another example of a solution (there are so many!) and then write a song entitled *"We're Better Together!"* In this song, be sure to discuss how you met, how you came together, and how you are composed. Describe why, as a team, you are better than you were when alone.	Playing with our food – we've all done it. Some of us have gotten in trouble for it! Mixing together all the stuff that's left over on the plate – eggs swirled with toast; mashed potatoes mixed with meatloaf. As much trouble as you may get into for that kind of playing around, did you know that some people actually get paid to do it? It's true! Rocky road ice cream, for example, is a combination of chocolate chips, nuts, and marshmallows. This type of "playing" also happens to perfectly illustrate the concept of a mixture. A *mixture* is a combination of two or more substances that do not lose their identifying characteristics when combined. Brainstorm a list of other examples of common "mixtures." You may include examples of products oriented toward people (like Chex® Mix) or animals (like Kibbles 'n' Bits®.)	A *compound* is the result of different atoms from two or more elements combining together in such a way that they cannot be separated again . . . so a new substance is formed. Water is a great, and very common, example of a compound. It is the combination of 2 hydrogen atoms with one oxygen atom. A form of sugar called sucrose ($C_{12}H_{22}O_{11}$ = 12 carbons + 22 hydrogens + 11 oxygens) is another common compound. The *atoms* from the individual elements combine to form a new *molecule* of a compound. Research a wide variety of compounds, and write their chemical make-up on individual index cards. Now, as done in the card game WAR, pit them against one another, and see who wins. The larger molecule wins!

Trees

Overview: *These Think-Tac-Toe options allow students to explore different aspects of trees: their parts and characteristics, their uses, and some famous trees.* By selecting one option from each row, students address each of these areas, but they are given choice regarding specific topics and products. Use this Think-Tac-Toe with a whole class, giving all students a chance to explore trees, or use it with a few students who might need enrichment during a study of plants.

Standards:
  ➢ Build an understanding of plant growth and adaptation
  ➢ Build an understanding of the interdependence of plants and animals

Objectives:
The students will **KNOW**
  • Types of trees.
  • Parts of trees.
  • Uses of trees.

The students will **UNDERSTAND THAT**
  • Trees have specific parts that enable them to survive.
  • Trees are an important natural resource that should be protected.

The students will **BE ABLE TO**
  • Name and describe the parts of trees.
  • Identify and describe different types of trees.
  • Explain the importance of trees to people and animals.
  • Conduct research.
  • Work independently.
  • Use planning strategies to complete projects.

Materials:
  • Paper, pencils, crayons, markers, paint

Closure: When they have completed their chosen products, students share them in small groups. As a whole group, have them brainstorm possible slogans to encourage others to protect and save trees.

Trees

Paint or draw a picture of your favorite tree. Include all of its parts, including (at least) leaves, branches, and its trunk. Then create a diagram of this tree and label its parts.	Write a poem about a tree. Your poem must have at least 12 lines. Be sure to use vocabulary related to trees. How can you use the parts of a tree in your poem?	Create a nature guide that shows illustrations of at least 5 different types of trees. What is unique about each tree? How can we tell different trees apart? Where can these trees be found?
Think of as many products as you can that we get from trees. Make a list of those things. Then write a thank you note to a tree expressing your gratitude for all that it gives us.	Research three different types of trees. Make a list showing each of the products that can be made from these trees. Based on your lists, which is the most valuable tree? Why?	"Interview" a tree that is in danger of being cut down. First, list questions to ask the tree, and then provide the tree's answers. What will the tree have to say about its importance and why it should <u>not</u> be cut down?
Where is the oldest tree in the world? What type of tree is it? How old is it said to be? Why do you think it has survived for so long? Create a short written report to answer these questions.	What is the tallest tree in the US? Where is it? What kind of tree is it? How does it compare to other trees? Draw a scale diagram of the tree that helps others understand just how tall this tree is.	Select five states and find out what their state trees are. Why were these trees selected by these states? What is their significance in these states? Create a chart that tells others about the trees and their importance to their states.

Notes

Learning Profile-Based Social Studies

Landforms and Bodies of Water

Overview: *These projects, based on Gardner's Multiple Intelligences, give students a chance to "show what they know" about landforms and bodies of water while working in ways that match their learning profile preferences.* Students choose a project to complete independently from the options provided. Their work can be used to assess their understandings of specific landforms and bodies of water at the end of a study of this topic.

Standards:
  ➢ Understand various physical characteristics of the environment
  ➢ Apply basic geographic concepts and terminology

Objectives:

The students will **KNOW**
  • Landforms (for example, *mountain, mountain range, hill, plateau, island, archipelago, cape, peninsula, isthmus,* and *valley*).
  • Bodies of water (for example, *river, stream, pond, lake, system of lakes, ocean, gulf, strait,* and *bay*).

The students will **UNDERSTAND THAT**
  • The physical environment is made up of different landforms and bodies of water.
  • Different places have different physical characteristics.

The students will **BE ABLE TO**
  • Identify and describe landforms and bodies of water.
  • Read maps.
  • Make simple maps.
  • Work independently.

Materials:

- A posted listing of the landforms and bodies of water that have been studied as well as at least one map showing different landforms and bodies of water (students can use these as references as they work on their projects)
- Green, brown, and blue clay
- Small Styrofoam trays (such as vegetable trays from grocery stores) or small pieces of thick cardboard
- Paper, pencils, markers, crayons
- Index cards

Closure: After students have had a chance to share their work with their classmates, either as a whole group or in small groups, the teacher can invite them to share their favorite landforms and bodies of water. Which ones do they like most and why? Where have they seen these landforms and bodies of water in real life? Do they know of any of them in their local area or state? Where are they and what are they called?

Landforms and Bodies of Water Project Options

 **The Builder**

Your task is to make models of landforms and bodies of water using green, brown, and blue clay. You will use small Styrofoam trays or pieces of cardboard as the bottom of your models, and each model must show both a landform and a body of water. You must make at least 3 models that show different landforms and bodies of water. You must also provide a short written description telling what each model shows.

 **The Publisher**

You have been asked to design a new book to teach children about landforms and bodies of water. Your task is to create the pages for the book, and your book must include at least 5 landforms and 5 bodies of water. Decide which landforms and bodies of water to include in your book. How can you use pictures and words to help children learn about the different landforms and bodies of water?

 **The Game Maker**

Games can be a great way to learn. Your job is to create a concentration/memory game about the landforms and bodies of water that we have studied. Using the index cards provided, write the name of each landform and body of water on separate cards and then draw accurate pictures of each one on separate cards. Be sure to include all the landforms and bodies of water that we have studied. Once you have finished making your game, play it with a classmate!

Option #4

The Map Maker

Wow! A bunch of new islands (an archipelago!) have been discovered, and it is your job to create maps of each one. Explorers have traveled across each island and have provided brief, written descriptions of them. These descriptions are provided below. Use the descriptions to create simple maps of the islands. First, you will have to create simple symbols to show each landform and body of water. For example, what symbol can you use to show a mountain? What about a river? Oh, by the way, you get to name the islands, too!

Island #1 is shaped a lot like a circle and has a system of lakes, 2 mountains, and a peninsula.

Island #2 is bigger than Island #1 (but not much) and is shaped like a triangle. It has 5 rivers, a plateau, and a mountain range.

Islands #3 and **#4** are both shaped like squares, and they are very close to one another. Between them is a strait. **Island #3** has 4 ponds and a plateau. **Island #4** has a 3 mountains and a valley.

Human, Capital, and Natural Resources

Overview: *These projects provide opportunities for students to work in ways that mirror their learning profile preferences while examining different types of economic resources.* Students complete one of the project options and can opt to work either independently or with partners. Prior to working on these projects, provide students with a solid understanding of the different types of economic resources – human, capital, and natural – and of the differences between needs and wants.

Standards:
> ➢ Demonstrate basic economic reasoning skills and an understanding of the economy
> ➢ Evaluate how people use resources to satisfy their wants and needs

Objectives:
The students will **KNOW**
- *Human resources* (workers) are people who work to produce goods and/or provide services.
- *Capital resources* are items produced to help create goods, such as buildings, tools, and machines.
- *Natural resources* are items provided by the earth that help produce goods, such as oil, wood, water, and coal.

The students will **UNDERSTAND THAT**
- Many economic resources are limited.
- Given that many economic resources are limited, it is important to use them wisely.

The students will **BE ABLE TO**
- Categorize economic resources.
- Evaluate the roles of resources.

Materials:
- The Lorax by Dr. Seuss
- Classroom resources, including texts and the Internet, for student research as needed

---

Closure: After completing their projects, the students can meet in random, mixed-learning profile groups to share their work. Then, pose the following questions to the whole group:

- What are the differences among human, capital, and natural resources?
- How are these resources related to one another?
- Which do you think are most important: human, capital, or natural resources? Why?
- What can happen when we don't have enough of a given resource?

Exploring Human, Capital, and Natural Resources Project Options

Option #1

_____ Read The Lorax by Dr. Seuss. Then list and categorize all of the resources included in the story. Which ones are human resources? Capital resources? Natural resources? Now brainstorm some real-world examples of these types of resources. Using your brainstorming as a starting point, write a new story that seeks to teach the same lesson that The Lorax teaches but does so using real-world resources and issues.

Option #2

_____ Brainstorm at least ten examples of each of the three types of economic resources (human, capital, and natural). Then select one from each category, and create a conversation in which each of the resources discusses its role and importance. What would each resource type say about its importance and its role in our lives? Finally, write a short, written statement identifying which category of resources – human, capital, or natural – is most important, and defend your choice.

Option #3

_____ Select and research a major industry such as farming or the computer industry. Brainstorm and categorize, as human, capital, and natural, the resources that the industry relies on most heavily. Then, create a detailed diagram, using both pictures and words, that shows how the resources are interrelated within the industry. Next, create a cause and effect chart that shows what happens when one of these resources is not readily available.

Option #4

Brainstorm and research examples of human, capital, and natural resources that can be found in your state. Once you have six to eight resources for each category, rank order in terms of importance the resources on each list, and pick the one resource from each list that you think is most important to your state. Write a statement that clearly expresses the reasons you picked it. When you have finished, you should have a total of three written statements, one for each type of resource.

U.S. States

Overview: *These projects allow students to work either independently or with others to synthesize what they know and understand about the geographic, economic, and historic elements that define any given state in the United States.* The project options are based on Gardner's Theory of Multiple Intelligences. Students choose projects based upon their learning profiles and choose to work alone or with a partner. The teacher also has the flexibility of allowing students to complete projects in small groups of no more than four students. Decide how many projects each student must complete. These projects ask students to apply their understandings of the many aspects that make each U.S. state unique and, thus, they can be used as an evaluation of the students' learning.

Standards:
- Demonstrate knowledge of the geography and regions of a given state
- Demonstrate knowledge of the early settlers of a given state and their interaction with the state's environment
- Demonstrate knowledge of the role a given state played in the history and development of the United States as a nation
- Demonstrate knowledge of the government and economics of a given state
- Describe and compare physical and cultural characteristics of the regions of a given state
- Examine the role that ethnic groups have played in the development of a given state and the impact of various cultural groups on the state
- Identify and assess the role of prominent persons in a given state, past and present

Objectives:
The students will **KNOW**
- The location of different geographic regions within a given state.
- Important historical events that occurred in a given state.
- The forms of exchange that have been used to purchase goods throughout a given state's history.

The students will **UNDERSTAND THAT**
- Geographic regions have distinctive characteristics that determine the location and type of human interaction.
- Native American Indians inhabited much of the current United States before European settlers arrived in a given area and contributed to an area's culture.

- Immigration and migration alter the ethnic and cultural make-up of a given state's population.
- Cultural landscapes reflect beliefs, customs, and architecture of the people of any given state.
- Individuals from a given state have made important contributions to the history of the United States as a country.
- Natural resources, industry, technology, transportation, and the growth of cities contribute to a given state's economy.

The students will **BE ABLE TO**

- Analyze and interpret maps to explain relationships among landforms and water features.
- Name and locate the geographic regions of a given state.
- Compare and contrast historical events as they contributed to a given state's development.
- Interpret ideas and events from different historical perspectives.
- Make connections between past and present events in a given state.
- Sequence events in a state's history.
- Identify prominent individuals that have contributed to the state and nation's history.
- Describe and compare the cultural characteristics of regions within a given state and evaluate their significance.
- Determine cause and effect relationships.

Materials: (depending on the projects chosen by the students)

- Access to the Internet
- Atlas, maps of the given state
- Reference and library books about the given state
- Chosen material for map design
- Examples of different poetry types
- Chosen material for flag design
- Travel brochures about the state (AAA is a good source for these)
- Paper and art supplies
- Method to record songs

Closure: If these projects are used as a major culminating event for a study of a particular state, the teacher may want to provide time for each of the students to share his or her project with the class (and, perhaps, parents, administrators, and/or other classes). Other options include creating a class "state museum" in order to display the students' work or allowing the students to share their products in small groups.

U.S. State Project Options

The Map Maker

You are designing a unique and original map of your state. The map can be two or three-dimensional, and you may choose what format or material you will use to construct your map.

For example, your map might be designed on felt or fabric, on poster board or plywood, on a sheet cake, or generated on the computer. Let your imagination be your guide as to what materials you use to create your map. Remember that your map must be easy to read and inviting for people to study. The following information must be clearly displayed on your map:

- ✓ Major cities in your state
- ✓ Large rivers and lakes
- ✓ Natural resources (if found)
- ✓ Mountain ranges (if applicable)
- ✓ The geographic regions of your state
- ✓ The most important products produced by your state and the locations where they are produced
- ✓ Any other optional information you feel is important to your state

The Poet

You have been given the task of composing a collection of poems that convey important information about your state. Your collection must include at least 4 different types of poems. The poems can describe important people from your state, a historical event that took place in your state, products or resources found in your state, places of interest in your state, etc. After reading each poem, the reader should learn a piece of information about your state. You may choose from the following types of poems:

✓ Alliterative poem	✓ Haiku	✓ Cinquain
✓ Narrative poem	✓ Acrostic poem	✓ Shape or concrete poem
✓ Rhyming poem	✓ Alphabet poem	✓ Diamante

The Flag Maker

Read about your state flag in an encyclopedia, a book about your state, a site on the Internet, or any other reliable source of your choice. In a short paragraph, describe what the figures, symbols, and colors mean on the real flag of your state.

After reading about and researching your state, design a new flag that, in your opinion, shows more clearly what is important about or important to your state.

Choose the material to construct an actual model of your new state flag. You must be able to explain why you chose the symbols, figures, etc. that you include on your flag when you share it with your classmates. You do not have to actually sew your flag. You may draw a picture of it on poster board, use pieces of felt, use foam board, etc.

The Advertising Executive

You have been hired by your state to design a new travel brochure that entices people from all over the United States and the World to visit your state. Include in the brochure both written descriptions and pictures. The illustrations can be drawn, generated on a computer, or carefully cut from magazines, pamphlets, etc. Your job is to design and construct an example of this brochure. Your main objective is to convince travelers that your state is the one to visit out of all the fifty United States.

(Note: If the teacher is comfortable with this option, he or she may also allow or encourage students to create a webpage with the same requirements.)

The Researcher

Every state has its funny, strange, or wacky incidents and stories. Use the Internet and reference materials to research any unusual facts or events related to your state. To share these with your classmates, compile them into a book entitled <u>Strange but True Facts About</u> _____ *(your state.)* You may use the word processor to print the pages of your book, or you can design it by hand. Place only one fact on each page, and add an illustration about the fact. The last step is to bind the book pages together in a manner of your choice.

Search for wacky, interesting, or strange facts from your state about:

- ✓ agriculture (crops, livestock, etc.)
- ✓ weather
- ✓ awards, medals
- ✓ parks, amusement centers
- ✓ colleges, universities
- ✓ population information
- ✓ corporations, businesses
- ✓ sports
- ✓ discoveries, inventions
- ✓ laws and documents
- ✓ elections
- ✓ memorable dates
- ✓ famous people
- ✓ flags, names, mottoes
- ✓ landmarks
- ✓ any other information you discover
- ✓ disasters

The Composer

Compose original lyrics to a song that could become the new State Song for your state. The lines to the song should rhyme and reflect places, people, products, values, or history that are important to your state.

You may choose the tune to a song that you already know, or, if music is your strength, you may compose your own tune. You can present your song to the class by either singing the song or recording it and playing it to the class, but you must also have a written product to share which shows the song's lyrics.

The Chef

You have been selected to prepare a meal for the governor of your state. The menu for this dinner must include foods and dishes typical of your state. Only use foods grown, raised, or produced in your state. Spices or other ingredients may come from elsewhere.

Plan the dishes to serve at this dinner. Design and construct a special menu to give to each person who attends the dinner and that explains why each food was selected. Include the following dishes on the menu:

- ✓ Appetizer
- ✓ Soup
- ✓ Salad
- ✓ Entree or entrees (the main dish)
- ✓ Vegetables
- ✓ Dessert
- ✓ Drinks

Choose at least one of the dishes to be served to the class and include the recipe for preparing it.

The Author

Take your reader on an unexpected trip through your state by composing a story told through the eyes of a small animal. This animal accidentally lands aboard a vehicle that is touring your state. The vehicle can be a car, van, camper, motorcycle, bus, etc. Explain in your story how this animal accidentally came to take this trip. What humans, if any, are in the vehicle with your animal? Do the humans know that the animal is along? If so, how do they interact with this character?

Your job is to pick out important points of interest that your character and his companions visit on their journey. Plan your trip in a logical order so that the visitors are not jumping back and forth from one side of the state to the other. Include short descriptions of the points of interest that they visit. Talk about the climate at several locations, and have your animal character describe the sights and sounds that surround him or her.

Make the ending of your story happy by returning the animal to its home. Use any illustrations that you feel are appropriate. You may draw them by hand, generate them on the computer, or cut out pictures from magazines or travel brochures.

The American Revolution

Overview: *These learning profile-based RAFT assignments give students an opportunity to apply their knowledge of the causes of the American Revolution, key figures and events of the period, and the colonists' responses to England.* Students complete their chosen tasks either individually or with partners, and it is left to the teacher to decide how many RAFT assignments each student completes.

Standards:
- ➢ Examine the causes, effects, and consequences of the American Revolution
- ➢ Describe the roles and impacts of key individuals during this period
- ➢ Describe key events that occurred during the American Revolution

Objectives:

The students will **KNOW**
- • The positions held by Loyalists and Patriots leading up to and during the American Revolution.
- • Key individuals and events important to the American Revolution.
- • The main causes of the American Revolution.

The students will **UNDERSTAND THAT**
- • Prior to the American Revolution, conflicts developed between the colonies and England over how the colonies would be governed.
- • The Declaration of Independence provided reasons for independence and ideas for self-government.
- • Key figures in the American Revolution persuaded colonists to support one side or the other.
- • The American Revolution divided families.

The students will **BE ABLE TO**
- • Sequence events in history.
- • Describe the impact that important figures had on the American Revolution.
- • Compare and contrast historical issues and events.
- • Interpret ideas and events from different historical perspectives.
- • Draw conclusions and make generalizations.

Materials:
- Reference materials about the American Revolution, including texts, primary documents located on the Internet, web sites, and resources from the media center
- Art materials to produce cards, time lines and sketches

Closure: Create mixed-learning profile groups, including a variety of different RAFT options in each, and allow time for the students to share their work in these smaller groups. While in these groups, the students debate the most important events and figures in the American Revolution.

The American Revolution

ROLE	AUDIENCE	FORMAT	TOPIC
Colonists dressed as Indians who threw crates of tea into the Boston Harbor	The crates of tea that were dumped into the harbor	Song sung by the colonists to explain why they destroyed the tea	Yo Ho, Yo Ho, We're Drowning the Tax on Tea
The editor of the <u>Virginia Gazette</u> newspaper	Virginia colonists	Editorial	Why the American Colonies Must Fight for Their Independence from England
Declaration of Independence	Thomas Jefferson	Thank you card	Because You Created Me, Here are the Reasons Why I'll Be Remembered Forever
A Patriot Soldier fighting for independence	His father, a wealthy landowner	Personal letter	How I Can Convince You to Give Up Your Loyalty to England and Join the Patriot's Cause
General Washington	The Continental Congress	A time line	Five Important Battles of the Revolution with the Dates and Locations Where They Occurred
Patrick Henry	The Virginia General Assembly	A persuasive speech	The Five Most Important Reasons Why We Must Separate from England
A colonial artist expressing why forming a new government is important to him	Benjamin Franklin, a member of the Continental Congress	A sketch	A New Flag for Our New Nation
A Patriot	His brother, a Loyalist	A poem	We Are Tearing Our Family Apart!

American Indian Tribes and Culture

<u>**Overview**</u>: *These Think-Tac-Toe options allow students to choose their own ways of showing what they have come to know and understand about the history, culture, and impact of American Indian tribes.* The tasks are structured according to Gardner's Theory of Multiple Intelligences. Students choose any three options in the grid. Use this Think-Tac-Toe as one of the culminating activities for a unit on American Indian life both past and present and combine it with other formal assessments to evaluate student learning. The teacher has the option of applying these tasks to local American Indian tribes within a given state or broadening the study to include tribes across the United States.

Standards:
  - ➢ Describe how American Indians in the past adapted to the climate and their environment to secure food, clothing, and shelter
  - ➢ Analyze the interactions between European settlers and the American Indian people, including the contributions of the Indians to the survival of the settlers
  - ➢ Examine national identities, religious beliefs, customs, and various folklore traditions of American Indian tribes
  - ➢ Describe the economy and systems of government within American Indian tribes

Objectives:
The students will **KNOW**
  - • The kinds of food American Indians ate, the clothing they wore, and the shelters that they used.
  - • The identities, religious beliefs, culture, customs, and folklore of given American Indian tribes.
  - • The effects of trade between American Indians and European settlers, and the impact trade had on the native economies.

The students will **UNDERSTAND THAT**
  - • American Indians interacted with the climate and their environment to meet their basic needs.
  - • American Indian peoples and the European settlers established trading relationships which led to either positive or negative interactions.
  - • Each American Indian tribe had its own unique identity, religious beliefs, culture, customs, and folklore.

- The American Indian traditions, food, and knowledge of survival in the environment became a part of the lives of the European settlers.

The students will **BE ABLE TO**

- Compare and contrast American Indian life and culture with the life and culture of the European settlers.
- Describe how given American Indian tribes adapted their existence to their natural environment (how they obtained food, clothing, tools, etc.).
- Identify the religious beliefs, culture, customs, food, and folklore of given American Indian tribes.
- Draw conclusions and make generalizations.
- Make inferences.
- Interpret ideas and events from different cultural perspectives.

Materials: (depending upon the activity chosen)

- Access to the Internet
- Reference materials about American Indian tribes that are a part of your state's standard course of study
- Bulletin board paper or other large paper
- Markers, crayons, paint
- Poster board or tag board
- A drum or object that can approximate a drum
- Copies of the Think-Tac-Toe

Closure: Encourage students to share their work either in small groups or with the whole class. Then, they can work in small, randomly-assigned groups to create lists titled *"The Top Five Contributions American Indians Have Made to American Culture."*

American Indian Tribes and Culture

Create a dictionary of words and phrases that had their beginnings in an American Indian language but have since become part of our English vocabulary. Using the Internet as a valuable resource, include the tribe from which the word came, if possible, along with its definition. Type into your search engine *"Native American words found in English."* Each dictionary entry should include the word or phrase, its meaning, its use in a sentence, and information about its origin. (verbal/linguistic)	Choose an American Indian tribe that your class has studied. Using a large piece of paper, such as bulletin board paper, design and create a mural of a typical village scene illustrating daily life in your chosen tribe. Your mural should show the tribe's dress, shelter/housing, daily activities, the environment in which the tribe lived, and any other information you want to include. Your visuals may be hand-drawn or taken from the Internet or magazines and glued onto the mural (or a combination of both).You must draw the background environment. (visual/spatial)	Assume the role of an American Indian trader from the tribe of your choice. You have learned to speak English. Write a dialogue between yourself and a European trader. Discuss what your tribe has to trade that the Europeans would want and also what your tribe needs from the Europeans. Include in the dialogue whether or not the trade was successful. You will need to research what trade items were important to both sides. (interpersonal)
Choose an American Indian tribe that your class has studied. Design and create a chart that compares and contrasts life in the tribe with life in a European settlement in the same area. Include dress, shelter, protection and weapons, food, religion, and customs in your chart, along with any other areas of interest to you. Display the chart for your classmates to see. (mathematical/logical)	American Indians were experts in using the natural environment to help their tribes survive. After choosing a tribe that your class has studied, research the roles that landforms, bodies of water, weather, and native animals played in the survival of the tribe. Compose a set of instructions that will help an Indian child your age understand how to use these natural elements so that your tribe will survive. (naturalist)	Choose an American Indian tribe that your class has studied. Research the main way the tribe obtained food (hunting, farming, or gathering). Your tribe is having trouble getting food because of a drought, lack of animals, etc. Create a dance to offer to the Great Spirit, asking for help in obtaining food. Perform the dance for your class. You may use a drum to provide rhythm. (bodily/kinesthetic, rhythmic)
Music was very important in the lives of American Indians, especially during their celebrations. Using a tribe that your class has studied, choose a celebration that was important to this tribe, and create a melody appropriate to the celebration. You may hum or sing your melody to the accompaniment of a drumbeat. (musical/rhythmic)	Assume the role of a boy or girl your age living in an American Indian tribe that your class has studied. Compose a journal entry describing one day in your life as a part of this tribe. Include how you feel about being a part of this tribe and the duties given to you. Is your life easy or hard? Explain why in your journal. (intrapersonal)	Assume the role of an American Indian from the tribe of your choice. You speak no English, but are trying to communicate information about your tribe to the European settlers. Design a symbol representing your tribe to show to these settlers. Include as many details about your tribe as possible in the symbol. (visual/spatial, interpersonal)

ASSESSING LEARNING IN A DIFFERENTIATED CLASSROOM

Not everything that can be counted counts,
and not everything that counts can be counted. - **Albert Einstein**

Several years ago, one of us attended a presentation titled "Differentiation and Assessment" at a national conference. Clearly this was a topic that many other conference attendees considered to be important, for the large presentation room was packed. Teachers, parents, consultants, researchers, and university faculty from all around the country filled the room and left no seats available. A young graduate student, who was also the presenter, soon entered the room in a flurry of overheads and nervous energy. As she entered, she looked around and muttered, "I really don't know what to say about this." As it turned out, she really didn't have to say much. She showed two overheads on the screen. The first announced the title of the presentation; the other offered equally little: a simple quote about grading. That was all she had time to show before the audience erupted.

The attendees expressed a wide array of concerns about grades and testing. They described instances in which students had been treated unfairly in the assessment process. They pointed out how seemingly impossible and time-consuming it is to create rubrics, which themselves had to be differentiated. They worried about how difficult it is to remove the subjective aspects of grading from what, at least in theory, should be largely objective in nature. The members of the audience raised some important issues. And no consensus was reached. At the end of the hour, they left the room feeling just as frustrated and confused as when they had entered. The graduate student was left holding the remainder of her overheads and wondering where the time had gone.

Assessment is a "sticky wicket" in any classroom. This is true whether we differentiate or not. Certainly at the elementary school level, we can all recall at least one occasion in which a student turned in a project or an assignment that had the looks of some rather heavy "parent assistance." Perhaps the project looked a little too crisp and clear, the handwriting a tad too straight or perfect, or maybe the contents of the assignment reflected a knowledge that seemed a little beyond this third grader's background. When we try to judge this work for a *grade* against another student's, one whose poster may not be quite so picture perfect, it is difficult to decide how to phrase this distinction -- and then deduct for it.

Many times there are simply no easy answers to the problems assessment presents, maybe even more so as we consider it within the context of differentiation. Add to this the very real nature of high-stakes, state testing which is becoming, more and more, the focus of school districts across the country, and we may well begin to feel a sense of anxiety about how to best and accurately assess progress in our classrooms and in our schools. That being said, we do believe that there are ways to make assessment more effective and efficient, even within the complex process of differentiation.

When we work with teachers and the topic of grading crops up (and it *always* does), we begin the discussion by asking everyone to consider the purposes of grades.

Why do we have them? What are they supposed to do? While the specific word choice may vary, the answers to these questions are always the same: "They communicate information to students, parents, and teachers about how a student is doing in a particular subject." "They tell us what the students 'got' during a unit of study." "Grades let us as teachers know how well we've taught the material in a unit of study." Indeed these are valid ways of thinking about the role of grades.

But we'd like to add to these ideas that grades also provide teachers with an opportunity to see what skills or knowledge students are still missing. Herein lies the primary difference between assessment in a traditional classroom environment and assessment in a differentiated one. In the former, it serves as an ending, like the close of a chapter in that portion of study during the school year. In a differentiated learning environment, it is both an ending point and a beginning point.

Assessment in a differentiated classroom must be ongoing and flexible. This is particularly true in an elementary classroom where, as we have all witnessed, a student suddenly turns a corner on a challenging skill and experiences a dramatic learning growth spurt. Assessment should serve as the foundation for instructional decision making. As stated in Chapter 1, the cycle of assessment and instruction in a differentiated classroom ensures that each student is offered opportunity for both challenge and success with the tasks she is given. Grading and assessment are not simply the "events" that occur at the end of each unit or marking period. This is, of course, a tall order. But it does not mean that we have to throw out our grade books. It means, instead, that we must adjust or modify both the ways we *collect* data about our students and the ways we *use* that data to plan our instruction. To this end, we offer some tips for getting the most out of classroom assessment.

1) **Pre-assess wisely**. Often teachers give a unit pre-assessment and then fail to use what they learn from it. The temptation to ignore the results of a pre-assessment is strong. We as teachers – constantly squeezed by the pressures of grading, designing lessons, communicating with parents, and a host of other responsibilities – might feel that reviewing pre-assessments is just another time-consuming task we must do. It is one that is easy to skip. Don't! We advise giving yourself time to use what you learn by giving a pre-assessment one to two weeks before a unit begins. This gives you ample time to check the pre-assessments and analyze the results. Are there some items that all or no students missed? Are there items for which there is a wide range of responses? Did the results of the pre-assessment indicate to you that there are portions of the upcoming unit where everyone seems weak? Conversely, did the results show you areas of strength for the group as a whole? Knowing the answers to questions such as these helps you plan your unit accordingly. The time it takes to go through this process might very well be saved in skipping material that the bulk of your students already know. And being able to anticipate those areas where there are indicated weaknesses helps you plan more efficiently the depth and breadth of your unit.

2) **Never reinvent the wheel**. This one is simple: If your curriculum resources provide assessments, use them as pre-assessments. A unit post-test from that math or language arts textbook chapter can easily serve as your pre-assessment, and it can be used again at the end of the unit along with other forms of assessment. Similarly, ask fellow teachers

for samples of quizzes and tests they have created over the years. Share and share alike. Many schools have created file cabinets or places where teachers of a common grade level can place copies of materials and assessments they use.

3) **Focus only on the objectives you really need to assess**. An assessment tool need only be detailed enough to let the teacher know whether or not a student has met the objectives being highlighted at that particular time. For example, when critiquing a product you might consider only the qualities of "neatness," "spelling," and "use of color" rather than the full gambit of skills ranging from "punctuation" to "effective discussion of content." Particularly for younger students, limiting the criteria for evaluation can yield more fruitful results. On that same note, when asking students to evaluate their own work, rather than having them judge a particular category on a scale of 1 to 10, you might simply employ a system of "faces," from the frowny to the smiley. By keeping the assessment process simple and objective-focused, the assessment is more likely to provide the kind of information we really need at a particular point and allows students to focus on building a few skills at a time rather than tackling what might otherwise seem to be an overwhelming number of them.

4) **Assess frequently and quickly**. There are certainly times in our instruction when a lengthy, deep assessment is needed, and students need to learn how to prepare for and take these types of assessments. However, there are other times when a "short and sweet" assessment can be highly effective. Because assessment drives instruction in a differentiated classroom and because teachers generally don't have much extra time for additional grading, we suggest that you consider assessing frequently but that you also keep most of your assessment tools fairly short and focused. In an elementary school classroom, these "short and focused" assessment opportunities might be as simple as sitting down with a small group and having a conversation about the material that has been explored thus far in the unit. Well-selected questions and a sharp ear for the answers can yield just as much information as a pencil and paper quiz and are much easier to "grade." Short "checkpoints" throughout a unit help to ensure that students are progressing and meeting the necessary objectives along the way. The "3-2-1" strategy is great for quickly finding

out what students have grasped during a lesson or activity. A teacher might ask students to do the following on index cards a few minutes before finishing the science lesson:

> **3:** Identify and describe 3 sources of water.
>
> **2:** Explain 2 ways that water moves from one location to another in the water cycle.
>
> **1:** Write 1 question you still have about the water cycle.

A quick review of the index cards should give the teacher a good idea of what the students understand and what they need more work with in regards to the water cycle.

5) **Vary assessment formats.** Most teachers of young students have figured this one out early on in their career: There are only so many pencil and paper tests students can handle before the class rebels. Elementary teachers excel at "mixing it up" when it comes to instruction, and this same creative spirit can certainly be applied to assessment. Allowing students to show what they know, understand, and can do in a variety of different ways over the course of a unit gives them the opportunity to practice different skills while showing what they have learned. The reality, of course, is that many of our students have to take the state-mandated test near the end of the year, and it is multiple-choice. So, of course, they should be asked to complete some multiple-choice assessments along the way. This is, after all, the best and *only* way they can learn the strategies needed for taking them successfully. However, mix multiple-choice tests with other formats, including more informal assessments such as journal entries and graphic organizers. Keep in mind that, in the end, teachers are interested in knowing how well students know and understand the material so that they can use that information in their own planning. If the students do not grasp the material initially, they will never be successful when asked to take that standardized state assessment. To this end, give students a wide variety of ways to show you what they know. Consider some alternate (and equally informative) forms of assessment.

Some "In the Box" Assessments	*Some "Out of the Box" Assessments*
Tests	Cartoons
Quizzes	Interviews/conversations
Worksheets	Graphic organizers
Book reports	Journal entries
Essays	Maps
Homework	Brown bag collections
Short answer questions	Bulletin "discussion" boards

Opportunities for assessment abound. What this really means is to consider almost everything that happens in a classroom potentially useful as assessment data.

6) **Involve students in assessment**. Brain research tells us that a great deal of learning occurs when students are asked to evaluate their own work. Plus, having students involved in assessment has some practical benefits for teachers as well. It could mean that the teacher does not have to grade every product but instead can take a more cursory look at some of them (but certainly not all). Here is a great trick that works well with Think-Tac-Toes: (Do not tell the students this up front!) When they have each completed their Think-Tac-Toe products (assume for the sake of illustration that they have each completed a total of three), ask each student to pick one product for *you* to evaluate, one for another student to evaluate, and one that they evaluate. Everyone can use the same assessment tool, such as a rubric or checklist, for the evaluations, but now, instead of having to grade three products from each student, the teacher is grading only one. In our experience, students are often much harder on themselves than teachers are when it comes to assigning a grade to their work. It is also a good idea to involve students in the creation of the assessment tool itself. Asking students to design product rubrics and checklists serves two important purposes: 1) It gives them a chance to review information and skills that they have learned, and 2) it helps to ensure that they meet the evaluation criteria by giving them increased ownership of it.

7) **Don't grade everything**. Usually when we say this to a group of teachers, everyone gasps. This might go against the grain for most professional educators, but, yes, we are suggesting that you resist at times the temptation to formally assess everything that you ask your students to do. You are probably saying to yourself right now, "If we don't grade it, will they do it?" Perhaps not. Which is why we don't advise giving an assignment and then telling the students that you will not be grading it. By the time they reach the fourth or fifth grade, students have had ample time to figure out how to play the game – and grades are certainly a part of that game. But the fact is that much of what we do with our students ought to be done for practice and preparation for something bigger (perhaps a test or project) and, in that sense, practices really should not be graded. Think back to the sports metaphor we began with in Chapter 1. Practices in sports serve to build skills and confidence. They prepare players for something bigger – a game or match. The same could be said for practice activities in classrooms, and this need for practice can certainly be communicated to students. We certainly believe that teachers should not ask students to complete work that is unnecessary, and we do not want students to think that because we are not grading it, it is not important. But even young students are capable of under-standing that some classroom tasks are building blocks needed for the "bigger picture."

8) **Keep records!** So much of what we learn about students cannot be boiled down to a number or a letter. How can we record in a grade book a brilliant comment or, alterna-tively, a major gap in thinking? *Qualitative* data is as important as, if not more important than, *quantitative* data. For this reason, we advise designing an efficient way to maintain a paper trail of your observations in the classroom and of students' comments. Whether it is a sticky pad that you carry with you at all times, a page of mailing labels that can be added to a file folder later, or a simple pad of paper, you will be glad you have those notes when report card and parent conference times roll around.

As we envisioned this book, we wrestled with this chapter a bit. Certainly, a topic as important as this one – assessment in a differentiated classroom – could have been the first chapter in this book because, at the end of the day, assessment really is a starting point for differentiation. Frankly, the first eleven chapters in this book, the "doing something" chapters, are of little importance and use without assessment. Differentiating instruction is an on-going cycle of assessing, planning, assessing again, and adjusting until we find the right fit for our students. Regardless of how you choose to do it, effective differentiation cannot happen without a thoughtful and purposeful approach to assessment.

RESOURCES

Armstrong, Thomas (2003). *The Multiple Intelligences of Reading and Writing: Making Words Come Alive.*

Bender, William N. (2002). *Differentiating Instruction for Students with Learning Disabilities.*

Benjamin, Amy (2003). *Differentiated Instruction: A Guide for Elementary School Teachers.*

Burke, Kay (1999). *How to Assess Authentic Learning.*

Coil, Carolyn (1997). *Teaching Tools for the 21st Century.*

Coil, Carolyn (2004). *Standards-Based Activities and Assessments for the Differentiated Classroom.*

Eidson, Caroline, Iseminger, Bob, & Taibbi, Chris (2007). *Demystifying Differentiation in Middle School: Tools, Strategies, & Activities to Use NOW.*

Heacox, Diane (2002). *Differentiating Instruction in the Regular Classroom: How to Reach and Teach All Learners, Grades 3-12.*

Meador, Karen (2005). *Tiered Activities for Learning Centers: Differentiation in Math, Language Arts, Science & Social Studies.*

Northey, Sheryn S. (2005). *Handbook on Differentiated Instruction for Middle and High Schools.*

Silver, Harvey F., Strong, Richard W., & Perini, Matthew J. (2000). *So Each May Learn: Integrating Learning Styles and Multiple Intelligences.*

Tomlinson, Carol A. (1999). *The Differentiated Classroom: Responding to the Needs of All Learners.*

Tomlinson, Carol A., & Allen, Susan D. (2000). *Leadership for Differentiating Schools & Classrooms.*

Tomlinson, Carol A. (2001). *How to Differentiate Instruction in Mixed-Ability Classrooms.*

Tomlinson, Carol A., & Eidson, Caroline C. (2003). *Differentiation in Practice: A Resource Guide for Differentiating Curriculum, Grades K-5.*

Tomlinson, Carol A., & Eidson, Caroline C. (2003). *Differentiation in Practice: A Resource Guide for Differentiating Curriculum, Grades 5-9.*

Tomlinson, Carol A., & Strickland, Cindy A. (2005). *Differentiation in Practice: A Resource Guide for Differentiating Curriculum, Grades 9-12.*

Winebrenner, Susan (1992). *Teaching Gifted Kids in the Regular Classroom.*

Winebrenner, Susan (1996). *Teaching Kids with Learning Difficulties in the Regular Classroom.*

Wormeli, Rick (2006). *Fair Isn't Always Equal: Assessing & Grading in the Differentiated Classroom.*

About the Authors

Caroline C. Eidson

has co-authored three previous books about curriculum differentiation, including *Demystifying Differentiation in Middle School*, and speaks regularly on the topic to elementary, middle-school, and high-school teachers at local, state, and national levels as well as to pre-service teachers in undergraduate and graduate programs. She earned her doctorate in Educational Psychology at the University of Virginia and has taught and administrated in public and private schools for over 14 years. Caroline co-founded a school for gifted learners, led another school's accreditation efforts, and has served on school evaluation teams. She also designed and continues to teach web-based courses on curriculum differentiation. Other staff development expertise includes curriculum development, classroom management, concept-based teaching, and educating gifted learners. She has several publications in the field of gifted education.

Bob Iseminger

co-authored the book *Demystifying Differentiation in Middle School* and has over 25 years of experience in public education as a classroom teacher, math resource teacher, and coordinator of a magnet center for gifted education. He has worked in both urban and suburban settings at the elementary and middle school levels and in a consulting capacity with high school students. During his classroom career, Bob was named Teacher of the Year by his local district. He is a member of the adjunct staff at Hollins University where he has taught methods classes in the Masters of Teaching program. For ten years, he taught gifted licensure courses for the state of North Carolina. Bob currently serves as a consultant for schools and school districts at the state and national level with an emphasis on differentiation and gifted education.

Chris Taibbi

co-authored the book *Demystifying Differentiation in Middle School* and has 12 years of experience in public education as a classroom teacher in both urban and suburban settings. Chris worked in a full-time center for gifted education at the elementary level. At the middle school level, Chris served as a contracted after-school mentor for inner-city students. With Bob, Chris has been part of a co-teaching team at Hollins University where they have taught methods classes in the Masters of Teaching program. Chris has also served as a consultant for school districts in North Carolina and Virginia with an emphasis on differentiation and gifted education and taught gifted licensure classes for eight years for the state of North Carolina. For the past four years, Chris has taught English at the secondary level in Roanoke, Virginia.